French
Phrasebook

BROCKHAMPTON PRESS
LONDON

© 1995 Geddes & Grosset Ltd,
David Dale House, New Lanark, Scotland.

This edition published 1995 by Brockhampton Press,
a member of the Hodder Headline PLC Group.

ISBN 1 86019 062 6

4 6 8 10 9 7 5 3

Printed and bound in India

CONTENTS

CONTENTS

KEY TO PRONUNCIATION

Guide to French pronunciation scheme

ah	as in bad, far, father
ai	as in met, excuse, well, mercy
ay	as in obey, day
aw	as in hot, blot, fought
ee	as in meal, feel, souvenir
er	as in the, tick, speaker
ew	as in beautiful*
oo	as in true, blue, glue
oh	as in note, boat

* There is no exact equivalent in English for the French 'closed' oo sound. Try with your lips to make the oo shape, while saying the ee sound through them.

The other area of French pronunciation without exact equivalents in English is the ng sounds, reduced here for simplicity to two:

an	as in French comprend (sounds like ong, as in song)
ern	as in French bien (sounds like ang, as in bang)

French consonants are pronounced much as in English.

GETTING STARTED

Everyday words and phrases

Yes
Oui
wee

No
Non
non

Please
S'il vous plaît
seel voo play

Yes, please
Oui, s'il vous plaît
wee, seel voo play

No, thank you
Non, merci
non, mair-see

Thank you
Merci
mair-see

Good
Bien
byern

OK
Ça va
sah vah

Excuse me
Excusez-moi
aiks-kew-say-mwah

I am very sorry
Je suis désolé
jer swee day-soh-lay

Being understood

I do not understand
Je ne comprends pas
jer ner kohm-pran pah

I understand
Je comprends
jer kohm-pran

Being understood

Do you understand?
Comprendez-vous?
kohm-prer-nay-voo

I do not speak French
Je ne parle pas français
jer ner pahrl pah fran-say

Do you speak English?
Parlez-vous anglais?
par-lay-voo zan-glay

Can you help me, please?
Pouvez-vous m'aider, s'il vous plaît?
poo-vay-voo may-day, seel voo play

Could you repeat that?
Pourriez-vous répétez, s'il vous plaît?
poo-ryay-voo ray-pay-tay, seel voo play

Please repeat that slowly
Répétez lentement, s'il vous plaît
ray-pay-tay lan-ter-man, seel voo play

Please write it down
Notez-le, s'il vous plaît
noh-tay-ler, seel voo play

Can you translate this for me?
Pouvez-vous me traduire ceci?
poo-vay-voo me trah-dweer ser-see

Can you find someone who speaks English?
Y a-t-il quelqu'un qui parle anglais?
ee-ah-teel kail-kern kee pahrl an-glay

Greetings and exchanges

Please point to the phrase in the book
Montrez-moi la phrase dans le livre, s'il vous plaît
mon-tray mwah la frahz dan ler leevr, seel voo play

It does not matter
Ce n'est rien
ser nai ryern

I do not mind
Ça ne me dérange pas
sa ner mer day-ranj pah

Greetings and exchanges

Hello
Bonjour
bon-joor

Hi
Salut
sah-lew

Good morning
Bonjour
bon-joor

Good evening
Bonsoir
bon-swahr

How are you?
Comment allez-vous?
koh-man tah-lay voo

Greetings and exchanges

I am very well, thank you
Très bien, merci
trai byern, mair-see

It is good to see you
Je suis heureux de vous voir
jer swee zer-rer der voo vwahr

It is nice to meet you
Heureux de faire votre connaissance
her-rer der fair vohtr koh-nay-sans

That is very kind of you
Vous êtes très aimable
voo zait trai zai-mahbl

You are very kind
Vous êtes bien aimable
voo zait byern ay-mahbl

You are very welcome
Je vous en prie
jer voo zan pree

Good night
Bonne nuit
bohner nwee

Goodbye
Au revoir
oh rer-vwahr

See you soon
A bientôt
ah byern-toh

Greetings and exchanges

My name is…
Je m'appelle
jer mah-pail

What is your name?
Comment vous appelez-vous?
koh-man voo zah-play voo

Here is my son
Voici mon fils
vwah-see mon fees

   This is — my daughter
      Voici — ma fille
vwah-see — mah fee

            — my husband
            — mon mari
            — mon mah-ree

            — my wife
            — ma femme
            — mah fahm

I am on holiday
Je suis en vacances
jer swee zan vah-kans

I am a student
Je suis étudiant
jer swee zay-tew-dyan

I live in London
J'habite à Londres
jah-beet ah londr

Greetings and exchanges

I am from — Britain
   Je suis — Britannique.
 jer swee — bree-tah-neek

   — England
   — Anglais.
   — *ang-lay*

   — Scotland
   — Ecossais.
   — *zay-koh-say*

   — Wales
   — Gallois.
   — *gahl-wah*

   — Ireland
   — Irlandais.
   — *zeer-lan-day*

   — America
   — Américain.
   — *zah-may-ree-kern*

   — Australia
   — Australien.
   — *zoh-strah-lyern*

   — South Africa
   — Sud-Africain.
   — *sewd-ahf-ree-kern*

   — New Zealand
   — Néo-Zélandais.
   — *nayoh-zay-lan-day*

Common questions

Where?
Où?
oo

How?
Comment?
koh-man

Where is...?
Où se trouve   ?
oo ser troov...

How much?
Combien?
kohm-byern

Where are...?
Où se trouvent   ?
oo ser troov...

Who?
Qui?
kee

When?
Quand?
kan

Why?
Pourquoi?
poor-kwah

What?
Quoi?
kwah

Which?
Lequel?
ler-kail

Have you got any change?
Avez-vous de la monnaie?
ahvay voo der lah moh-nay

How long will it take?
Il y en a pour combien de temps?
eel-yohn-ah poor kohm-byern der tan

How much do I have to pay?
Combien dois-je payer?
kohm-byern dwah-jer pay-yay

Common questions

What do you call this in French?
Comment appelez vous ceci en français?
koh-man tah-play voo ser-see an fran-say

What does this mean?
Que veut dire ceci?
ker ver deer ser-see

What is the problem?
Quel est le problème?
kail ai ler proh-blaim

What is this?
Qu'est-ce que c'est?
kais-ker say

What is wrong?
Qu'est-ce qui ne va pas?
kais-kee ner vah pah

What time do you close?
A quelle heure fermez-vous?
ah kail err fair-may voo

Where can I change my clothes?
Où puis-je me changer?
oo pwee-jer mer shan-gay

Who did this?
Qui a fait cela?
kee ah fay ser-lah

Who should I see about this?
A qui puis-je m'adresser?
ah kee pwee-jer mah-drai-say

Where can I buy a postcard?
Où puis-je acheter une carte postale?
oo pwee-jer ahsh-tay ewn kahrt pohs-tahl

How can I contact my American Express / Diners Club?
Comment puis-je contacter American Express/Diners Club?
koh-man pwee-jer kon-tahk-tay ah-may-ree-kan aik-sprais /
dee-nairs kloob

Do you know a good restaurant
Connaissez-vous un bon restaurant?
koh-nai-say voo zern bon rais-toh-ran

Do you mind if I…?
Est-ce que ça vous dérange si   ?
ais-ker sah voo day-ranj see...

May I borrow your map?
Puis-je emprunter votre plan?
pwee-jer an-prern-tay vohtr plan

Asking the time

What time is it?
Quelle heure est-il?
kail err ay-teel

It is…
Il est
eel ai

a quarter past ten	**a quarter to eleven**
dix heures et quart	onze heures moins le quart
dee-zerr ay kahr	*on-zerr mwan ler kahr*

Asking the time

after three o'clock
après trois heures
ah-prai trwah zerr

at about one o'clock
vers une heure
vair ewn err

at half past six
à six heures et demie
ah see-zerr ay der-mee

at night
la nuit
lah nwee

before midnight
avant minuit
ah-van mee-nwee

early
de bonne heure
der bohn err

eleven o'clock
onze heures
onz err

five past ten
dix heures cinq
deez err sank

five to eleven
onze heures moins cinq
onz err mwan sank

half past eight exactly
huit heures et demie tapantes
weet err zai der-mee tah-pant

half past ten
dix heures et demie
deez err zai der-mee

in an hour's time
dans une heure
dan zewn err

in half an hour
dans une demi-heure
dan zewn der-mee err

late
tard
tahr

midnight
minuit
mee-nwee

nearly five o'clock
presque cinq heures
praisk sank err

soon
bientôt
byern-toh

ten o' clock
dix heures
dee zerr

Common problems

ten past ten
dix heures dix
dee zerr dees

ten to eleven
onze heures moins dix
on zerr mwan dees

this afternoon
cet après-midi
sait ah-prai mee-dee

this evening
ce soir
ser swahr

this morning
ce matin
ser mahtern

tonight
cette nuit
sait nwee

twelve o'clock (midday)
midi
mee-dee

twenty-five past ten
dix heures vingt-cinq
dee zerr vern-sank

twenty to eleven
onze heures moins vingt
onz err mwan vern

two hours ago
il y a deux heures
eel ee ah derr zerr

Common problems

I have no currency
Je n'ai pas d'argent liquide
jer nay pah dahr-jan lee-keed

I have dropped a contact lens
J'ai laissé tomber un verre de contact
jay lay-say tohm-bay ern vair der kon-tahkt

I cannot find my driving licence
Je ne trouve pas mon permis de conduire
jer ner troov pah mon pair-mee der kon-dweer

Common problems

I have lost my credit cards
J'ai perdu mes cartes de crédit
jay pair-dew may kahrt der kray-dee

I must see a lawyer
Je veux voir un avocat
jer ver vwahr ern ah-voh-kah

My car has been stolen
On m'a volé ma voiture
on mah voh-lay mah vwah-tewr

My handbag has been stolen
On m'a volé mon sac
on mah voh-lay mon sahk

My wallet has been stolen
On m'a volé mon portefeuille
on mah voh-lay mon pohrt-fery

Arrival

Here is my passport
Voici mon passeport
vwah-see mon pahs-pohr

We have a joint passport
Nous avons un passeport conjoint
noo zah-von ern pahs-pohr kon-jwern

I am attending a convention
Je participe à une convention
jer pahr-tee-seep ah ewn con-van-syon

I am here on business
Je suis ici pour affaires
jer swee zee-see poor ahf-air

I will be staying here for eight weeks
Je reste huit semaines
jer raist wee ser-main

We are visiting friends
Nous sommes chez des amis
noo sohm shay day-zah-mee

I have nothing to declare
Je n'ai rien à déclarer
jer nay ryern ah day-klah-ray

I have the usual allowances
J'ai les quantités permises
jay lay kan-tee-tay pair-meez

Arrival

This is for my own use
C'est pour mon usage personnel
sai poor mon ew-sahj pair-soh-nail

Common problems and requests

I have lost my ticket
J'ai perdu mon billet
jay pair-dew mon bee-yay

I have lost my traveller's cheques
J'ai perdu mes chèques de voyage
jay pair-dew may shaik der vohy-ahj

I have missed my connection
J'ai raté ma correspondance
jay rah-tay mah koh-rais-pon-dans

The people who were to meet me have not arrived
Les gens qui devaient venir me chercher ne sont pas arrivés
lay jan kee der-vay ver-neer mer shair-shay ner son pah zah-ree-vay

I am in a hurry
Je suis pressé
jer swee prai-say

I am late
Je suis en retard
jer swee zan rer-tahr

Where will I find the airline representative?
Où est l'agent de la compagnie aérienne?
oo ai lah-jan der lah kon-pah-nee ai-ree-ain

Common problems and requests

I have lost my bag
J'ai perdu mon sac
jay pair-dew mon sahk

Where can I buy currency?
Où puis-je changer de l'argent?
oo pwee-jer shan-jay der lahr-jan

Where can I change traveller's cheques?
Où puis-je changer des chèques de voyage?
oo pwee-jer shan-jay day shaik der vohy-ahj

Where is — the bar?
Où est — le bar?
oo ai — ler bahr

— the lounge?
— le salon d'attente?
— ler sah-lon dah-tant

— the toilet?
— les toilettes?
— lay twah-lait

— the transfer desk?
— le guichet de transit?
— ler gee-shay der tran-see

— the information desk?
— le bureau de renseignements?
— ler bew-roh der ran-sain-yer-man

Is there a bus into town?
Y a-t-il un autobus pour aller en ville?
ee-ah-teel ern oh-toh-bews poor ah-lay an veel

Common problems and requests

Can I upgrade to first class?
Puis-je prendre un billet de première classe?
pwee-jer prandr ern bee-yay der prer-mee-air klahs

Where do I get the connection flight to Nice?
Où dois-je prendre la correspondance pour Nice?
oo dwah-jer prandr lah koh-rais-pon-dans poor nees

Luggage

Where is the baggage from flight number…?
Où sont les bagages du vol numéro ?
oo son lay bah-gahj dew vohl new-may-roh...

My baggage has not arrived
Mes valises ne sont pas arrivées
may vah-leez ner son pah zah-ree-vay

Where is my bag?
Où est mon sac?
oo ai mon sahk

   It is — a large suitcase
C'est — une grande valise
   sai — tewn grand vah-leez

          — a rucksack
          — un sac à dos
          — tern sahk ah doh

          — a small bag
          — une petite valise
          — tewn per-teet vah-leez

Luggage

These bags are not mine
Ces sacs ne sont pas à moi
say sahk ner son pah ah mwah

Where do I pick up my bags?
Où reprend-on ses bagages?
oo rer-pran-ton say bah-gahj

Are there any baggage trolleys?
Y a-t-il des chariots à bagages?
ee-ah-teel day shah-ryoh ah bah-gahj

Can I check in my bags?
Puis-je enregistrer mes bagages?
pwee-jan-ray-jees-tray may bah-gahj

Can I have help with my bag?
Y a-t-il un porteur?
ee-ah-teel ern pohr-terr

Careful, the handle is broken
Attention, la poignée est cassée
ah-tan-syon, lah pwah-nyay ai kah-say

This package is fragile
Ce paquet est fragile
ser pah-kay ai frah-jeel

I will carry that myself
Je porterai ceci moi-même
jer pohr-tai-ray ser-see mwah-maim

Is there a left-luggage office?
Y a-t-il une consigne?
ee-ah-teel ewn kon-seen

Luggage

Is there any charge?
Faut-il payer?
foh-teel pay-yay

No, do not put that on top
Non, ne mettez pas ça en haut
non, ner mai-tay pah sah ohn-oh

Please take these bags to a taxi
Portez ces valises à un taxi, s'il vous plaît
pohr-tay say vah-leez ah ern tahk-see, seel voo play

AT THE HOTEL

Reservations and enquiries

My name is…
Je m'appelle
jer mah-pail

I have a reservation
J'ai réservé
jay ray-sair-vay

I am sorry I am late
Je suis en retard Excusez-moi
jer swee zan rer-tahr. aiks-kew-say mwah

I was delayed at the airport
J'ai été retenu à l'aéroport
jay ay-tay rer-ter-new ah lahee-roh-pohr

My flight was late
Mon vol avait du retard
mon vohl ah-vay dew rer-tahr

I shall be staying until July 4th
Je reste jusqu'au quatre juillet
jer raist jews-koh kahtr joo-yay

I want to stay for 5 nights
Je veux rester cinq nuits
jer ver rais-tay sank nwee

There are five of us
Nous sommes cinq
noo sohm sank

Reservations and enquiries

Do you have — a single room?
  Avez-vous — une chambre pour une personne?
  ah-vay voo — zewn shanbr poor ewn pair-sohn

       — a double room with a bath?
       — une chambre pour deux personnes
          avec bain?
       — zewn shanbr poor der pair-sohn
          ah-vaik bern

       — a room with twin beds and a shower?
       — une chambre avec lits jumeaux et douche?
       — zewn shanbr ah-vaik lee jew-moh ay doosh

I need — a double room with a bed for a child
Je veux — une chambre pour deux personnes avec un lit
      d'enfant
jer ver — ewn shanbr poor der pair-sohn ah-vaik ern lee dan-fan

       — a room with a double bed
       — une chambre avec un grand lit
       — ewn shanbr ah-vaik ern gran lee

       — a room with twin beds and bath
       — une chambre avec lits jumeaux et bain
       — ewn shanbr ah-vaik lee jew-moh ay bern

       — a single room
       — une chambre pour une personne
       — ewn shanbr poor ewn pair-sohn

       — a single room with a shower or bath
       — une chambre pour une personne avec douche ou bain
       — ewn shanbr poor ewn pair-sohn ah-vaik doosh oo bern

Reservations and enquiries

Does the price include — room and breakfast?
Est-ce que le tarif comprend — la chambre et le petit
                                                      déjeuner?
*ais-ker ler tah-reef kohm-pran — lah shanbr ay ler per-tee
                                                      day-jer-nay*

                            — room and all meals?
                            — la chambre et tous les repas?
                            — lah shanbr ay too lay rer-pah

                            — room and dinner?
                            — la chambre et le dîner?
                            — la shanbr ay ler dee-nay

How much is it — for a child?
Combien coûte — pour un enfant?
kohm-byern koot — poor ewn an-fan

                            — per night?
                            — par nuitée?
                            — pahr nwee-tay

                            — per person?
                            — par personne?
                            — pahr pair-sohn

How much is — full board?
Combien coûte — la pension complète?
kohm-byern koot — lah pan-syon kohm-plait

                            — half-board?
                            — la demi-pension?
                            — lah der-mee pan-syon

Reservations and enquiries

Which floor is my room on?
A quel étage est ma chambre?
ah kail ay-tahj ai mah shanbr

Can we have breakfast in our room?
Pouvons-nous prendre le petit déjeuner dans la chambre?
poo-von noo prandr ler per-tee day-jer-nay dan la shanbr

Is this a safe area?
Est-ce que la région est sûre?
ais-ker lah ray-jeeon ai sewr

Can we have adjoining rooms?
Pouvons-nous avoir des chambres attenantes?
poo-von noo zah-vwahr day shanbr za-ter-nant

Are there other children staying at the hotel?
Y a-t-il d'autres enfants à l'hôtel?
ee-ah-teel dohtr zan-fan ah loh-tail

Are there supervised activities for the children?
Y a-t-il des activités surveillées pour les enfants?
ee-ah-teel day zahk-tee-vee-tay sewr-vay-yay poor lay zan-fan

Can my son sleep in our room?
Est-ce que mon fils peut dormir avec nous?
ais-ke mon fees per dohr-meer ah-vaik noo

Is the voltage 220 or 110?
Est-ce que le courant est à 220 ou 110 volts?
ais-ker ler koo-ran ai ah der san van oo san dee vohlt

Is there a trouser press I can use?
Puis-je faire repasser mon pantalon?
pwee-jer fair rer-pah-say mon pan-tah-lon

Reservations and enquiries

Is there — a television?
Y a-t-il — un poste de télévision?
ee-ah-teel — ern pohst der tay-lay-vee-syon

      — a hairdryer?
      — un sèche-cheveux?
      — ern saish-sher-ver

      — a minibar?
      — un minibar?
      — ern mee-nee-bahr

      — a room service menu?
      — un menu servi dans les chambres?
      — ern mer-new sair-vee dan lay shanbr

      — a telephone?
      — un téléphone?
      — ern tay-lay-fohn

      — a casino?
      — un casino?
      — ern kah-see-noh

      — a lift?
      — un ascenseur?
      — ern ah-san-serr

      — a sauna?
      — un sauna?
      — ern soh-nah

      — a swimming pool?
      — une piscine?
      — ewn pee-seen

Reservations and enquiries

Do you have— a cot for my baby?
Avez-vous — un lit d'enfant pour mon bébé?
ah-vay voo — zan lee dan-fan poor mon bay-bay

> **— a laundry service?**
> — un service de blanchisserie?
> *— zern sair-vees der blan-shee-ser-ree*

> **— a car park?**
> — un parking?
> *— zern pahr-keeng*

> **— a safe for valuables?**
> — un coffre pour les objets de valeur?
> *— ern kohfr poor lay-zohb-jay der vah-lerr*

> **— a fax machine?**
> — un télécopieur?
> *— zern tay-lay-koh-pee-err*

Is there — a market in the town?
Y a-t-il — un marché en ville?
ee-ah-teel — ern mahr-shay an veel

> **— a Chinese restaurant?**
> — un restaurant chinois?
> *— ern rais-toh-ran sheen-wah*

> **— a Vietnamese restaurant?**
> — un restaurant vietnamien?
> *— ern rais-toh-ran vyait-nah-myern*

Do you have satellite TV
Recevez-vous les programmes par satellite?
rer-ser-vay voo lay proh-grahm pahr sah-tay-leet

Service

What time — does the hotel close?
A quelle heure — est-ce que l'hôtel ferme?
ah kail err — ais-ker loh-tail fairm

— does the restaurant close?
— ferme le restaurant?
— fairm ler rais-toh-ran

— is breakfast?
— est le petit déjeuner?
— ai ler per-tee day-jer-nay

— is lunch?
— est le déjeuner?
— ai ler day-jer-nay

— is dinner?
— est le dîner?
— ai ler dee-nay

— does the bar open?
— ouvre le bar?
— oovr ler bahr

Service

Please fill the minibar
Remplissez le minibar, s'il vous plaît
ran-plee-say ler mee-nee-bahr, seel voo play

Please send this fax for me
Transmettez ce fax, s'il vous plaît
trans-mai-tay ser fahks, seel voo play

Service

Please turn the heating off
Fermez le chauffage, s'il vous plaît
fair-may ler shoh-fahj, seel voo play

Please, wake me at 7 o'clock in the morning
Réveillez-moi à sept heures, s'il vous plaît
ray-vay-yay mwah ah sait err, seel voo play

  Can I have — an ashtray?
  Donnez-moi — un cendrier
doh-nay mwah — ern san-dree-ay

         — another blanket?
         — une autre couverture
         — ewn ohtr koo-vair-tewr

         — another pillow?
         — un autre oreiller
         — ern ohtr oh-ray-yay

         — my key, please?
         — ma clef, s'il vous plaît
         — lah klay, seel voo play

         — some coat hangers?
         — des cintres
         — day serntr

         — some note paper?
         — du papier
         — dew pah-pyay

         — a newspaper?
         — un journal?
         — an joor-nahl

Service

Can I have my wallet from the safe?
Donnez-moi mon portefeuille qui est au coffre?
doh-nay mwah mon pohrt-fery kee ai oh kohfr

Can I hire a portable telephone?
Puis-je louer un téléphone portatif?
pweej loo-ay ern tay-lay-fohn pohr-tah-teef

Can I make a telephone call from here?
Puis-je téléphoner d'ici?
pweej tay-lay-foh-nay dee-see

Can I send this by courier?
Puis envoyer ceci par coursier?
pweej an-vwah-yay ser-see pahr koor-syay

Can I use my charge card?
Puis-je utiliser ma carte de clientèle?
pweej ew-tee-lee-say mah kahrt der klee-an-tail

Can you connect me with the international operator?
Passez-moi la standardiste internationale?
pah-say mwah lah stan-dahr-deest an-tair-nah-syo-nahl

Can I have an outside line, please?
Passez-moi une ligne extérieure, s'il vous plaît
pah-say mwah ewn leen aiks-tair-yerr, seel voo play

Can you recommend a good local restaurant?
Pouvez-vous me recommander un bon restaurant?
poo-vay voo mer rer-koh-man-day ern bon rais-toh-ran

Can I charge this to my room?
Mettez cela sur ma note, s'il vous plaît
mai-tay ser-lah sewr mah noht, seel voo play

Service

Can I dial direct from my room?
Puis-je obtenir une ligne extérieure directement?
pweej ohb-ter-neer ewn leen aiks-tair-yerr dee-raik-ter-man

Can I use my personal computer here?
Puis-je utiliser mon PC ici?
pweej ew-tee-lee-say mon pay-say ee-see

I need an early morning call
Réveillez-moi de bonne heure
ray-vay-yay mwah der bohn err

     I need — some soap
 J'ai besoin — de savon
jay ber-zwern — der sah-von

           — some towels
           — de serviettes
           — der sair-vyait

           — a razor
           — d'un rasoir
           — dern rah-zwahr

I need some toilet paper
Il me faut du papier hygiénique
eel mer foh dew pah-pyay ee-jay-neek

I need to charge these batteries
Je veux recharger ces batteries
jer ver rer-shahr-jay say bah-ter-ree

I want to press these clothes
Je veux faire repasser ces vêtements
jer ver fair rer-pah-say say vait-man

Problems

Has my colleague arrived yet?
Est-ce que mon collègue est arrivé?
ais-ker mon koh-laig ai tah-ree-vay

How do I use the telephone?
Comment fait-on pour téléphoner?
koh-man fai-ton poor tay-lay-foh-nay

I am expecting a fax
J'attends un fax
jah-tan ern fahks

Where can I send a fax?
Où peut-on envoyer un fax?
oo per-ton an-vwah-yay ern fahks

What is the charge?
Quel est le tarif?
kail ai ler tah-reef

Problems

Can I speak to the manager?
Puis-je parler au directeur?
pweej pahr-lay oh dee-raik-terr

Where is the manager?
Où est le directeur?
oo ai ler dee-raik-terr

I cannot close the window
La fenêtre ne ferme pas
lah fer-naitr ner fairm pah

Problems

I cannot open the window
La fenêtre ne s'ouvre pas
lah fer-naitr ner soovr pah

The air conditioning is not working
La climatisation ne marche pas
lah klee-mah-tee-zah-syon ner mahrsh pah

The bathroom is dirty
La salle de bains est sale
lah sahl der bern ai sahl

The heating is not working
Le chauffage ne marche pas
ler shoh-fahj ner mahrsh pah

The light is not working
La lumière ne marche pas
lah lew-myair ner mahrsh pah

The room is not serviced
On ne fait pas le ménage dans la chambre
on ner fai pah ler may-nahj dan lah shanbr

The room is too noisy
La chambre est trop bruyante
lah shanbr ai troh broo-yant

The room key does not work
La clef de la chambre ne marche pas
lah klay der lah shanbr ner mahrsh pah

There are no towels in the room
Il n'y a pas de serviettes dans la chambre
eel nyah pah der sair-vyait dan lah shanbr

Checking out

There is no hot water
Il n'y a pas d'eau chaude
eel nyah pah doh shohd

There is no plug for the washbasin
Il n'y a pas de bonde dans le lavabo
eel nyah pah der bond dan ler lah-vah-boh

My daughter is ill
Ma fille est malade
mah fee ai mah-lahd

My son is lost
Mon fils s'est perdu
mon fees sai pair-dew

Checking out

Could you order me a taxi?
Appelez-moi un taxi, s'il vous plaît
ah-play mwah ern tahk-see, seel voo play

Please leave the bags in the lobby
Laissez les bagages dans le hall, s'il vous plaît
lay-say lay bah-gahj dan ler ahl, seel voo play

I want to stay an extra night
Je veux rester une nuit supplémentaire
jer ver rais-tay ewn nwee sew-play-man-tair

Do I have to change rooms?
Dois-je changer de chambre?
dwah jer shan-jay der shanbr

Checking out

Can I have the bill please?
Puis-je avoir la note, s'il vous plaît?
pweej ah-vwahr lah noht, seel voo play

We will be leaving early tomorrow
Nous partons tôt demain matin
noo pahr-ton toh der-mern mah-tern

Thank you, we enjoyed our stay
Merci, nous avons fait un bon séjour
mair-see, noo zah-von fai tern bon say-joor

OTHER ACCOMMODATION

Renting a house

We have rented this villa
Nous avons loué cette villa.
noo zah-von loo-ee sait vee-lah

Here is our booking form
Voici notre bon de réservation.
vwah-see nohtr bon der ray-sair-vah-syon

Can I contact you on this number?
Puis-je vous joindre à ce numéro?
pwee-jer voo jwandr ah ser new-may-roh

Can you send a repairman?
Pouvez-vous faire réparer?
poo-vay voo fair ray-pah-ray

How does this work?
Comment est-ce que ça marche?
koh-man ais-ker sah mahrsh

What is the voltage here?
Quelle est la tension, s'il vous plaît?
kail ai lah tan-syon, seel voo play

I cannot open the shutters
Les volets ne s'ouvrent pas.
lay voh-lay ner soovr pah

Is the water heater working?
Est-ce que le chauffe-eau marche?
ais-ker ler shoh-foh mahrsh

Renting a house

Is the water safe to drink?
Est-ce que l'eau est potable?
ais-ker loh ai poh-tahbl

Is there any spare bedding?
Y a-t-il de la literie de rechange?
ee-ah-teel der lah lee-ter-ree der rer-shanj

The cooker does not work
La cuisinière ne marche pas.
lah kwee-see-nyair ner mahrsh pah

The refrigerator does not work
Le frigidaire ne marche pas.
ler free-jee-dair ner mahrsh pah

The toilet is blocked
Les WC sont bouchés.
lay doobl-vay-say son boo-shay

There is a leak
Il y a une fuite.
eel-yah ewn fweet

We do not have any water
Nous n'avons pas d'eau.
noo nah-von pah doh

We need two sets of keys
Il nous faut deux jeux de clefs.
eel noo foh der jer der klay

When does the cleaner come?
Quand faites-vous le ménage?
kan fait voo ler may-nahj

Around the house

Where is — the fuse box?
  Où est — la boîte à fusibles?
  oo ai — lah bwaht ah few-zeebl

> **— the bathroom?**
> — la salle de bains?
> *— lah sahl der bern*

> **— the socket for my razor?**
> — la prise pour le rasoir?
> *— lah preez poor ler rah-zwahr*

> **— the key for this door?**
> — la clef de cette porte?
> *— lah klay der sait pohrt*

Around the house

bath
baignoire
bain-wahr

bathroom
salle de bains
sahl der bern

bed
lit
lee

brush
brosse
brohs

can opener
ouvre-boîte
oovr-bwaht

chair
chaise
shaiz

cooker
cuisinière
kwee-zee-nyair

corkscrew
tire-bouchon
teer-boo-shon

Around the house

cup
tasse
tahs

fork
fourchette
foor-shait

glass
verre
vair

kitchen
cuisine
kwee-zeen

knife
couteau
koo-toh

mirror
miroir
mee-rwahr

pan
casserole
kahs-rohl

plate
assiette
ass-yait

refrigerator
frigidaire
free-jee-dair

sheet
drap
drah

sink
évier
ay-vyay

spoon
cuillère
koo-yair

stove
cuisinière
kwee-see-nyair

table
table
tahbl

tap
robinet
roh-bee-nay

toilet
toilettes
twah-lait

vacuum cleaner
aspirateur
ahs-pee-rah-terr

washbasin
lavabo
lah-vah-boh

Camping

Can we camp in your field?
Pouvons-nous camper dans votre champ?
poo-von noo kan-pay dan vohtr shan

Can we camp near here?
Pouvons-nous camper près d'ici?
poo-von noo kan-pay prai dee-seé

Can we park our caravan here?
Pouvons-nous garer notre caravane ici?
poo-von noo gah-ray nohtr kah-rah-vahn ee-see

Please can we pitch our tent here?
Pouvons-nous planter notre tente ici?
poo-von noo plan-tay nohtr tant ee-see

Where do I pay?
Où dois-je payer?
oo dwah jer pay-yay

Do I pay when I leave?
Dois-je payer au départ?
dwah-jer pay-yay oh day-pahr

Is there a more sheltered site?
Y a-t-il un emplacement plus abrité?
ee-ah-teel ern an-plahs-man plew zah-bree-tay

Is there a restaurant or a shop on the site?
Y a-t-il un restaurant ou un magasin sur place?
ee-ah-teel ern rais-toh-ran oo ern mah-gah-zan sewr plahs

Camping

Is there another campsite near there?
Y a-t-il un autre terrain de camping près d'ici?
ee-ah-teel ern ohtr tair-ran der kan-peeng prai dee-see

Is this the drinking water?
Est-ce bien l'eau potable?
ais byern loh poh-tahbl

The site is very wet and muddy
L'emplacement est très humide et boueux.
lan-plahs-man ai trai zew-meed ay boo-er

Where are the toilets?
Où sont les toilettes?
oo son lay twah-lait

Where can I have a shower?
Où puis-je prendre une douche?
oo pweej prandr ewn doosh

Where can we wash our dishes?
Où pouvons-nous faire notre vaisselle?
oo poo-von noo fair nohtr vai-sail

Is there — a paddling pool?
Y a-t-il — une pataugeoire?
ee-ah-teel — ewn pah-toh-jwahr

— a swing park?
— des balançoires?
— day bah-lan-swahr

— a swimming pool?
— une piscine?
— ewn pee-seen

Around the campsite

air mattress
matelas pneumatique
maht-lah pner-mah-teek

backpack
sac à dos
sahk-ah-doh

bottle-opener
ouvre-bouteille
oovr-boo-tery

bucket
seau
soh

camp bed
lit de camp
lee der kan

camp chair
chaise pliante
shaiz plee-ant

candle
bougie
boo-jee

can-opener
ouvre-boîte
oovr-bwaht

cup
tasse
tahs

fire
feu
fer

flashlight
lampe électrique
lanp ay-laik-treek

fly sheet
double toit
doobl twah

folding table
table pliante
tahbl plee-ant

fork
fourchette
foor-shait

frying pan
poêle à frire
poh-ail ah freer

ground
sol
sohl

Around the campsite

ground sheet
tapis de sol
tah-pee der sohl

guy line
corde
kohrd

knife
couteau
koo-toh

mallet
maillet
mah-yay

matches
allumettes
ah-lew-mait

pail
seau
soh

penknife
canif
kah-neef

plate
assiette
ah-syait

rucksack
sac à dos
sahk ah doh

shelter
abri
ah-bree

sleeping bag
sac de couchage
sahk der koo-shahj

spoon
cuillère
koo-yair

stove
cuisinière
kwee-zee-nyair

tent
tente
tant

tent peg
piquet de tente
pee-kay der tant

tent pole
montant de tente
mon-tan der tant

thermos flask
bouteille thermos
boo-tery tair-moh

torch
lampe électrique
lanp ay-laik-treek

Hostelling

Are you open during the day?
Etes-vous ouvert pendant la journée?
ait voo zoo-vair pan-dan lah joor-nay

What time do you close?
A quelle heure fermez-vous?
ah kail err fair-may voo

Can we stay five nights here?
Pouvons-nous rester ici cinq nuits?
poo-von noo rais-tay ee-see sank nwee

Can we stay until Sunday?
Pouvons-nous rester jusqu'à dimanche?
poo-von noo rais-tay jews-kah dee-mansh

Do you serve meals?
Servez-vous des repas?
sair-vay voo day rer-pah

Can I use the kitchen?
Puis-me me servir de la cuisine?
pweej mer sair-veer der lah kwee-zeen

Here is my membership card
Voici ma carte de membre.
vwah-see mah kahrt der manbr

I do not have my card
Je n'ai pas ma carte sur moi.
jer nay pah mah kahrt sewr mwah

Hostelling

Can I join here?
Puis-je m'inscrire ici?
pweej mern-skreer ee-see

Thank you, we enjoyed our stay
Merci, nous avons fait un bon séjour.
mair-see, noo zah-von fai tern bon say-joor

Childcare

Can you warm this milk for me?
Pouvez-vous faire réchauffer ce lait, s'il vous plaît?
poo-vay voo fair ray-shoh-fay ser lai, seel voo play

Do you have a cot for my baby?
Avez-vous un lit d'enfant pour mon bébé?
ah-vay voo zan lee dan-fan poor mon bay-bay

Do you have a high chair?
Avez-vous une chaise haute?
ah-vay voo zewn shaiz oht

Is there a baby-sitter?
Y a-t-il une baby-sitter?
ee-ah-teel ewn bay-bay-see-tair?

My daughter is 7 years old
Ma fille a sept ans.
mah fee ah sait an

My son is 10 years old
Mon fils a dix ans.
mon fees ah dee zan

Childcare

She goes to bed at nine o'clock
Elle se couche à neuf heures.
ail ser koosh ah ner verr

We will be back in two hours
Nous serons de retour dans deux heures.
noo ser-ron der rer-toor dan der zerr

Where can I buy some disposable nappies?
Où puis-je trouver des couches à jeter?
oo pweej troo-vay day koosh ah jer-tay

Where can I change the baby?
Où puis-je changer le bébé?
oo pweej shan-jay ler bay-bay

Where can I feed my baby?
Où puis-je nourrir mon bébé?
oo pweej noo-reer mon bay-bay

I am very sorry. That was very naughty of him
Je suis désolé : il a été très vilain.
jer swee day-soh-lay : eel ah ay-tay·trai vee-lern

It will not happen again
Cela ne se reproduira pas.
ser-lah ner ser rer-proh-dwee-rah

GETTING AROUND

Asking for directions

Excuse me, please
Excusez-moi, s'il vous plaît
aik-skew-say mwah, seel voo play

Where is — the art gallery?
  Où est — la galerie d'art?
  oo ai — lah gah-lai-ree dahr

        — the police station?
        — le commissariat de police?
        — ler koh-mee-sah-ryah der poh-lees

        — the post office?
        — le bureau de poste?
        — ler bew-roh der pohst

Can you tell me the way to the bus station?
Où est la gare routière?
oo ai lah gahr roo-tyair

Can you show me on the map?
Montrez-moi sur le plan, s'il vous plaît
mon-tray mwah sewr ler plan, seel voo play

I am looking for the Tourist Information Office
Je cherche l'Office de Tourisme
jer shairsh loh-fees der too-reesm

I am lost
Je suis perdu
jer swee pair-dew

Asking for directions

I am lost. how do I get to the Hotel de la Gare?
Je suis perdu Où se trouve l'hôtel de la Gare?
jer swee pairdew. oo ser troov loh-tail der lah gahr

I am trying to get to the market
Je cherche le marché
jer shairsh ler mahr-shay

I want to go to the theatre
Je veux aller au théâtre
jer ver ah-lay oh tay-ahtr

Is this the right way to the supermarket?
C'est bien par ici, le supermarché?
sai byern pahr ee-see, ler sew-pair-mahr-shay

We are looking for a restaurant
Nous cherchons un restaurant
noo shair-shon zern rais-toh-ran

Where are the toilets?
Où sont les toilettes?
oo son lay twah-lait

Where do I get a bus for the city centre?
D'où part le bus pour le centre ville?
doo pahr ler bews poor ler santr veel

How long does it take to get to the park?
Il y en a pour combien de temps pour aller au parc?
eel yan ah poor kohm-byern der tan poor ah-lay oh pahrk

Is it far?
Est-ce loin?
ais lwern

Asking for directions

Can you walk there?
On peut y aller à pied?
on per tee ah-lay ah pyay

By road

Where does this road go to?
Où mène cette route?
oo main sait root

Which road do I take to Bordeaux?
Quelle est la route de Bordeaux?
kail ai lah root der bohr-doh

How do I get onto the motorway (highway)?
Comment rejoint-on l'autoroute (la grande route)?
koh-man rer-jwan ton loh-toh-root (lah grand root)

How far is it to Nancy?
Il y a combien de kilomètres jusqu'à Nancy?
eel yah kohm-byern der kee-loh-maitr jewsk-ah nan-see

How long will it take to get there?
Dans combien de temps y serai-je?
dan kohm-byern der tan ee ser-raij

I am looking for the next exit
Je cherche la prochaine sortie
jer shairsh lah proh-shain sohr-tee

Is there a filling station near here?
Y a-t-il un poste d'essence près d'ici?
ee-ah-teel ern pohst dai-sans prai dee-see

Directions

Which is the best route to Lyon?
Quelle est la meilleure route pour aller à Lyon?
kail ai lah mai-yerr root poor ah-lay ah lee-on

Which is the fastest route?
Quelle est la route la plus rapide?
kail ai lah root lah plew rah-peed

Directions

You go — left
Vous allez — à gauche
voo zah-lay — ah gohsh

— right
— à droite
— ah drwaht

— as far as...
— jusqu'à
— jewsk-kah

— towards...
— vers
— vair...

— around the corner
— juste à côté
— jewst ah koh-tay

Keep going straight ahead
Continuez tout droit
kon-tee-nway too drwah

Directions

Follow the signs for — the motorway
Suivez la direction — de l'autoroute
swee-vay lah dee-raik-syon — der loh-toh-root

— the next junction
— le prochain carrefour
— ler proh-shern kahr-foor

Turn left
Tournez à gauche
toor-nay ah gohsh

Turn right
Tournez à droite
toor-nay ah drwaht

It is — at the intersection
C'est — au carrefour
sai — toh kahr-foor

— next to the cinema
— à côté du cinéma
— ah koh-tay dew see-nay-mah

— on the next floor (up)/on the next floor (down)
— à l'étage au-dessus/à l'étage au-dessous
— ah lay-tahj oh der-sew/ ah lay-tahj oh der-soo

— opposite the railway station
— en face de la gare
— an fahs der lah gahr

— over there
— là-bas
— lah-bah

Hiring a car

You have to pay the toll
Il faut régler le péage
eel foh ray-glay ler pay-ahj

Take the first road on the right
Prenez la première à droite
prer-nay lah prer-myair ah drwaht

Take the road for Albi
Prenez la route d'Albi
prer-nay lah root dahl-bee

Take the second road on the left
Prenez la deuxième à gauche
prer-nay lah der-zyaim ah gohsh

Hiring a car

I want to hire a car
Je veux louer une voiture
jer ver loo-ay ewn vwah-tewr

Can I hire a car?
Puis-je louer une voiture?
pweej loo-ay ewn vwah-tewr

Can I hire a car with an automatic gearbox?
Puis-je louer une automatique?
pweej loo-ay ewn oh-toh-mah-teek

Can I pay for insurance?
Puis-je payer l'assurance?
pweej pay-yay lah-sew-rans

Hiring a car

Do I have to pay a deposit?
Dois-je verser des arrhes?
dwah-jer vair-say day zahr

Do I pay in advance?
Dois-je payer d'avance?
dwah-jer pay-yay dah-vans

Is tax included?
Est-ce que la taxe est comprise?
ais-ker lah tahks ai kohm-preez

Is there a charge per kilometre?
Y a-t-il un tarif par kilomètre?
ee-ah-teel ern tah-reef pahr kee-loh-maitr

Do you have— a large car?
Avez-vous — une grosse voiture?
ah-vay voo — zewn grohs vwah-tewr

— a smaller car?
— une voiture plus petite?
— zewn vwah-tewr plew per-teet

— an automatic?
— une automatique?
— zewn oh-toh-mah-teek

— an estate car?
— un break?
— zan braik

I need it for 2 weeks.
J'en ai besoin pour deux semaines
john ay ber-zwan poor der ser-main

Hiring a car

We will both be driving
Nous conduirons tous les deux
noo kohn-dwe-ron too lay der

I need to complete this form
Je dois remplir ce formulaire
jer dwah ran-pleer ser fohr-mew-lair

I want to leave the car at the airport
Je veux laisser la voiture à l'aéroport
jer ver lai-say lah vwah-tewr ah lai-roh-pohr

I would like a spare set of keys
Je voudrais un jeu de clefs de rechange
jer voo-drai ern jer der klay der rer-shanj

Must I return the car here?
Faut-il ramener la voiture ici?
foh-teel rahm-nay lah vwah-tewr ee-see

Please explain the documents
Expliquez-moi ces documents, s'il vous plaît
aiks-plee-kay mwah say doh-kew-man, seel voo play

Please show me how to operate the lights
Montrez-moi comment fonctionnent les phares
mon-tray mwah koh-man fon-syonn lay fahr

Please show me how to operate the windscreen wipers.
Montrez-moi comment fonctionnent les essuie-glace
mon-tray mwah koh-man fon-syonn lay ai-swee-glahs

Where is reverse gear?
Où est la marche arrière?
oo ai lah mahrsh ah-ryair

Hiring a car

Where is the tool kit?
Où est la trousse à outils?
oo ai lah troos ah oo-tee

How does the steering lock work?
Comment fonctionne l'antivol de direction?
koh-man fon-syohn lan-tee-vohl der dee-raik-syon

By taxi

Where can I get a taxi?
Où puis-je trouver un taxi?
oo pwee-jer troo-vay ern tahk-see

Please show us around the town
Faites-nous faire un tour de la ville, je vous prie
fait noo fair ern toor der lah veel, jer voo pree

Please take me to this address
Conduisez-moi à cette adresse, s'il vous plaît
kon-dwee-zay mwah ah sait ah-drais, seel voo play

How much is it per kilometre?
C'est combien le kilomètre?
sai kohm-byern ler kee-loh-maitr

Will you put the bags in the boot?
Mettez les valises dans le coffre, s'il vous plaît
mai-tay lay vah-leez dan ler kohfr, seel voo play

Please wait here for a few minutes
Attendez ici quelques minutes, s'il vous plaît
ah-tan-day ee-see kail-ker mee-newt, seel voo play

By taxi

Please, stop at the corner
Arrêtez-vous au coin, s'il vous plaît
ah-rai-tay voo oh kwern, seel voo play

Please, wait here
Veuillez patienter un moment
ver-yay pah-syan-tay an moh-man

Take me to the airport, please
Conduisez-moi à l'aéroport, s'il vous plaît
kon-dwee-zay mwah ah lai-roh-pohr, seel voo play

The bus station, please
La gare routière, s'il vous plaît
lah gahr roo-tyair, seel voo play

I am in a hurry
Je suis pressé
jer swee prai-say

Please hurry, I am late
Depêchez-vous, je suis en retard
day-pai-shay voo, jer swee zan rer-tahr

Turn left, please
Tournez à gauche, s'il vous plaît
toor-nay ah gohsh, seel voo play

Turn right, please
Tournez à droite, s'il vous plaît
toor-nay ah drwaht, seel voo play

Wait for me please
Attendez-moi, s'il vous plaît
ah-tan-day mwah, seel voo play

By taxi

Can you come back in one hour?
Pouvez-vous revenir dans une heure?
poo-vay voo rer-ver-neer dan zewn err

How much is that, please?
C'est combien, s'il vous plaît?
sai kohm-byern, seel voo play

Keep the change
Gardez la monnaie
gahr-day lah moh-nay

By bus

Does this bus go to the castle?
Est-ce que ce bus va au château?
ais-ker ser bews vah oh shah-toh

How frequent is the service?
Quelle est la fréquence du service?
kail ai lah fray-kans dew sair-vees

What is the fare to the city centre?
C'est combien pour le centre ville?
sai kohm-byern poor ler santr veel

When is the last bus?
Quand part le dernier bus?
kan pahr ler dair-nyay bews

Where do I get the bus for the airport?
D'où part le bus pour l'aéroport?
doo pahr ler bews poor lai-roh-pohr

Which bus do I take for the football stadium?
Quel bus faut-il prendre pour aller au stade?
kail bews foh-teel prandr poor ah-lay oh stahd

Will you tell me when to get off the bus?
Dites-moi où je dois descendre
deet mwah oo jer dwah day-sandr

By train

When is the next train to Calais?
Quand part le prochain train pour Calais?
kan pahr ler proh-shern trern poor kah-lay

Where can I buy a ticket?
Où puis-je acheter un billet?
oo pweej ash-tay ern bee-yay

Can I buy a return ticket?
Puis-je prendre un aller-retour?
pweej prandr ern ah-lay-rer-toor

A return (round-trip ticket) to Toulouse, please
Un aller-retour pour Toulouse, s'il vous plaît
ern ah-lay-rer-toor poor too-looz, seel voo play

A return to Paris, first class
Un aller-retour pour Paris, en première classe
ern ah-lay-rer-toor poor pah-ree, an prer-myair klahs

A single (one-way ticket) to Montpellier, please
Un aller simple pour Montpellier, s'il vous plaît
ern ah-lay-sernpl poor mon-per-lyay, seel voo play

By train

A smoking compartment, first-class
Compartiment fumeurs, première classe
kohm-pahr-tee-man few-merr, prer-myair klahs

A non-smoking compartment, please
Compartiment non-fumeurs, s'il vous plaît
kohm-pahr-tee-man non-few-merr, seel voo play

Second class. A window seat, please
Deuxième classe Côté fenêtre, s'il vous plaît
der-zyaim klahs. koh-tay fer-naitr, seel voo play

I have to leave tomorrow
Je dois partir demain
jer dwah pahr-teer der-man

I want to book a seat on the sleeper to Paris
Je veux réserver une couchette dans le train de Paris
jer ver ray-sair-vay ewn koo-shait dan ler trern der pah-ree

What are the times of the trains to Paris?
Quels sont les horaires des trains pour Paris?
kail son lay zoh-rair day trern poor pah-ree

Where is the departure board (listing)?
Où est le tableau des départs?
oo ai ler tah-bloh day day-pahr

Where should I change?
Où faut-il changer?
oo foh-teel shan-jay

Can I take my bicycle?
Puis-je emmener mon vélo?
pweej an-mer-nay mon vay-loh

By train

Is there — a restaurant on the train?
Y a-t-il — un restaurant dans le train?
ee-ah-teel — ern rais-toh-ran dan ler trern

> **— a buffet car (club car)?**
> — un buffet?
> *— ern bew-fay*

> **— a dining car?**
> — un wagon-restaurant?
> *— ern vah-gon rais-toh-ran*

Do I have time to go shopping?
Ai-je le temps de faire des courses?
ay-jer ler tan der fair day koors

Which platform do I go to?
C'est sur quel quai?
sai sewr kail kay

How long do I have before my next train leaves?
Il me reste combien de temps avant le prochain train?
eel mer raist kohm-byern der tan ah-van ler proh-shern trern

What time does the train leave?
A quelle heure part le train?
ah kail err pahr ler trern

What time is the last train?
A quelle heure part le dernier train?
ah kail err pahr ler dair-nyay trern

Where do I have to change?
Où faut-il changer?
oo foh-teel shan-jay

By train

Is this the Marseilles train?
C'est bien le train de Marseille?
sai byern ler trern der mahr-say

Is this the platform for Grenoble?
C'est bien le quai pour le train de Grenoble?
sai byern ler kay poor ler trern der grer-nohbl

Is this a through train?
Est-ce un train direct?
ais ern trern dee-raikt

Are we at Orléans yet?
Sommes-nous arrivés à Orléans?
sohm noo zah-ree-vay ah ohr-lay-an

What time do we get to Nantes?
A quelle heure arrivons-nous à Nantes?
ah kail err ah-ree-von noo zah nant

Do we stop at Le Mans?
Est-ce que le train s'arrête au Mans?
ais-ker ler trern sah-rait oh man

Are we on time?
Sommes-nous à l'heure?
sohm noo zah lerr

How long will the delay be?
Combien de temps faudra-t-il attendre?
kohm-byern der tan foh-drah-teel ah-tandr

How long will this take?
Il y en a pour combien de temps?
eel yan ah poor kohm-byern der tan

By train

Can you help me with my bags?
Pouvez-vous m'aider avec mes bagages?
poo-vay voo may-day ah-vaik may bah-gahj

I want to leave these bags in the left-luggage
Je veux laisser ces bagages à la consigne
jer ver lai-say say bah-gahj ah lah kon-seen

I shall pick them up this evening
Je reviendrai les prendre ce soir
jer rer-vyern-drai lay prandr ser swahr

How much is it per bag?
C'est combien par sac?
sai kohm-byern parh sahk

May I open the window?
Puis-je ouvrir la fenêtre?
pweej oov-reer lah fer-naitr

Is this seat taken?
Est-ce que cette place est libre?
ais ker sait plahs ai leebr

My wife has my ticket
C'est ma femme qui a mon billet
sai mah fahm kee ah mon bee-yay

I have lost my ticket
J'ai perdu mon billet
jay pair-dew mon bee-yay

This is a non-smoking compartment
C'est un compartiment non-fumeurs
sai tern kohm-pahr-tee-man non-few-merr

By train

This is my seat
C'est ma place
sai mah plahs

Where is the toilet?
Où sont les toilettes?
oo son lay twah-lait

Why have we stopped
Pourquoi avons-nous stoppé?
poor-kwah ah-von noo stoh-pay

DRIVING

Traffic and weather conditions

Are there any hold-ups?
Y a-t-il des bouchons?
ee-ah-teel day boo-shon

Is the traffic one-way?
Est-ce une route à sens unique?
ais ewn root ah sans ew-neek

Is the pass open?
Est-ce que le col est ouvert?
ais ker ler kohl ai too-vair

Is the road to Annecy snowed up?
Est-ce que la route d'Annecy est enneigée?
ais ker lah root dahn-see ai tan-nai-jay

Is the traffic heavy?
Y a-t-il beaucoup de circulation?
ee-ah-teel boh-koo der seer-kew-lah-syon

Is there a different way to the stadium?
Y a-t-il une autre route pour aller au stade?
ee-ah-teel ewn ohtr root poor ah-lay oh stahd

Is there a toll on this motorway (highway)?
Est-ce que cette autoroute (route) est à péage?
ais ker sait oh-toh-root (root) ai tah pay-ahj

What is causing this traffic jam?
Pourquoi y a-t-il un embouteillage?
poor-kwah ee-ah-teel ern an-boo-tery-ahj

Traffic and weather conditions

What is the speed limit?
Quelle est la limitation de vitesse?
kail ai lah lee-mee-tah-syon der vee-tais

When is the rush hour?
Quelles sont les heures de pointe?
kail son lay zerr der pwant

When will the road be clear?
Quand est-ce que la voie sera dégagée?
kan es ker lah vwah ser-ra day-gah-jay

Do I need snow chains?
Est-ce que j'ai besoin de chaînes?
ais ker jay ber-zwern der shain

Parking

Can I park here?
Puis-je me garer là?
pwee-jer mer gah-ray lah

Do I need a parking disc?
Ai-je besoin d'un disque de stationnement?
ai-jer ber-zwern dern deesk der stah-syonn-man

Do I need coins for the meter?
Faut-il mettre des pièces dans le parcmètre?
foh-teel maitr day pyais dan ler pahrk-maitr

Do I need parking lights?
Faut-il laisser les feux de position allumés?
foh-teel lai-say lay fer der poh-zee-syon ah-lew-may

At the service station

How long can I stay here?
Combien de temps puis-je stationner ici?
kohm-byern der tan pwee-jer stah-syonn-ay ee-see

Is it safe to park here?
Peut-on se garer ici sans risque?
per-ton ser gah-ray ee-see san reesk

What time does the car park close?
A quelle heure ferme le parking?
ah kail err fairm ler pahr-keeng

Where can I get a parking disc?
Où peut-on acheter un disque de stationnement?
oo per-ton ahsh-tay ern deesk der stah-syonn-man

Where is there a car park?
Est-ce qu'il y a un parking?
ais keel-yah ern pahr-keeng

At the service station

Fill the tank, please
Le plein, s'il vous plaît
ler plern, seel voo play

— 25 litres of 3 star
— 25 litres de super
— vernt-sank leetr der sew-pair

— 25 litres of 4 star
— 25 litres de super-plus
— vernt-sank leetr der sew-pair-plews

At the service station

— 25 litres of diesel
— 25 litres de gazole
— vernt-sank leetr der gah-zohl

— 25 litres of unleaded petrol
— 25 litres de sans plomb
— vernt-sank leetr der san plohm

Can you clean the windscreen?
Nettoyez le pare-brise, s'il vous plaît
nai-twah-yay ler pahr-breez, seel voo play

Check — the oil, please
Vérifiez — l'huile, s'il vous plaît
vay-ree-fyay — lweel, seel voo play

— the water, please
— l'eau, s'il vous plaît
— loh, seel voo play

— the tyre pressure, please
— les pneus, s'il vous plaît
— lay pner, seel voo play

The pressure should be 2.3 at the front and 2.5 at the rear
C'est 2,3 à l'avant et 2,5 à l'arrière
sai der trwah ah lah-van ay der sank ah lah-ryair

I need some distilled water
Il me faut de l'eau distillée
eel mer foh der loh dees-tee-lay

Do you take credit cards?
Acceptez-vous les cartes de crédit?
ahk-saip-tay voo lay kahrt der kray-dee

Breakdowns and repairs

Can you give me a can of petrol, please?
Avez-vous un bidon d'essence, s'il vous plaît?
ah-vay voo zern bee-don dai-sans, seel voo play

Can you give me — a push?
   Pouvez-vous — me pousser?
   poo-vay voo — mer poo-say

   — a tow?
   — me prendre en remorque?
   — mer prandr an rer-mohrk

Can you send a recovery truck?
Pouvez-vous envoyer une dépanneuse?
poo-vay voo zan-vwah-yay ewn day-pah-nurz

Can you take me to the nearest garage?
Pouvez-vous me conduire au garage le plus proche?
poo-vay voo mer kohn-dweer oh gah-rahj ler plew prohsh

I have run out of petrol
Je suis en panne sèche
jer swee zan pahn saish

Is there a telephone nearby?
Y a-t-il un téléphone près d'ici?
ee-ah-teel ern tay-lay-fohn prai dee-see

Do you have an emergency fan belt?
Avez-vous une courroie de secours?
ah-vay voo zewn koo-rwah der ser-koor

Breakdowns and repairs

Do you have jump leads?
Avez-vous un câble de démarrage?
ah-vay voo zan kahbl der day-mah-rahj

I have a flat tyre
J'ai un pneu crevé
jay ern pner krer-vay

I have blown a fuse
Un fusible a sauté
ern few-zeebl ah soh-tay

I have locked myself out of the car
Les clefs sont enfermées à l'intérieur
lay klay son tan-fair-may zah lan-tay-ryerr

I have locked the ignition key inside the car
La clef est enfermée à l'intérieur
lah klay ai tan-fair-may ah lan-tay-ryerr

I have lost my key
J'ai perdu ma clef
jay pair-dew mah klay

I need a new fan belt
Il me faut une courroie de ventilateur neuve
eel mer foh tewn koo-rwah der van-tee-lah-terr nerv

I think there is a bad connection
Je crois qu'il y a un mauvais contact
jer krwah keel yah ern moh-vai kohn-tahkt

Can you repair a flat tyre?
Pouvez-vous réparer un pneu crevé?
poo-vay voo ray-pah-ray ern pner krer-vay

Breakdowns and repairs

My car — has been towed away
Ma voiture — a été emmenée à la fourrière
mah vwah-tewr — ah ay-tay an-mer-nay ah lah foo-ryair

— has broken down
— est en panne
— ai tan pahn

— will not start
— ne démarre pas
— ner day-mahr pah

My windscreen has cracked
Mon pare-brise est fêlé.
mon pahr-breez ai fai-lay

The air-conditioning does not work
La climatisation ne marche pas
lah klee-mah-tee-zah-syon ner mahrsh pah

The battery is flat
Les accus sont à plat
lay zah-kew son tah plah

The engine has broken down
Le moteur est en panne
ler moh-terr ai tan pahn

The engine is overheating
Le moteur chauffe
ler moh-terr shohf

The exhaust pipe has fallen off
J'ai perdu mon pot d'échappement
jay pair-dew mon poh day-shahp-man

Breakdowns and repairs

There is a leak in the radiator
Il y a une fuite au radiateur
eel yah ewn fweet oh rah-dyah-terr

Can you replace the windscreen wiper blades?
Pouvez-vous changer les balais des essuie-glace?
poo-vay voo shan-jay lay bah-lay day zai-swee-glahs

There is something wrong
Il y a un problème
eel yah an proh-blaim

There is something wrong with the car
La voiture ne marche pas
lah vwah-tewr ner mahrsh pah

Is there a mechanic here?
Y a-t-il un mécanicien?
ee-ah-teel ern may-kah-nee-syern

Can you find out what the trouble is?
Savez-vous ce qui ne va pas?
sah-vay voo ser kee ner vah pah

Do you have the spare parts?
Avez-vous les pièces détachées?
ah-vay voo lay pyais day-tah-shay

Is it serious?
Est-ce grave?
ais grahv

Can you repair it for the time being?
Pouvez-vous faire une réparation temporaire?
poo-vay voo fair ewn ray-pah-rah-syon tan-poh-rair

Accidents and the Police

Will it take long to repair it?
Combien de temps faudra-t-il pour les réparations?
kohm-byern der tan foh-drah-teel poor lay ray-pah-rah-syon

Accidents and the Police

There has been an accident
Il y a eu un accident
eel ya ew ern ahk-see-dan

We must call an ambulance
Il faut appeler une ambulance
eel foh tah-play ewn an-bew-lans

We must call the police
Il faut appeler la police
eel foh tah-play lah poh-lees

What is your name and address?
Quel est votre nom et votre adresse?
kail ai vohtr nohm ay vohtr ah-drais

You must not move
Ne bougez pas
ner boo-jay pah

He did not stop
Il ne s'est pas arrêté
eel ner sai pah zah-rai-tay

He is a witness
Il est témoin
eel ai tay-mwan

Accidents and the Police

He overtook on a bend
Il a doublé dans un virage
eel ah doo-blay dan zern vee-rahj

He ran into the back of my car
Il m'a embouti à l'arrière
eel mah an-boo-tee ah lah-ryair

He stopped suddenly
Il s'est arrêté brusquement
eel sai tah-rai-tay brewsk-man

He was moving too fast
Il roulait trop vite
eel roo-lay troh veet

Here are my insurance documents
Voici mes pièces d'assurance
vwah-see may pyais dah-sew-rans

Here is my driving licence
Voici mon permis de conduire
vwah-see mon pair-mee der kon-dweer

How much is the fine?
Quel est le montant de la contravention?
kail ai ler mon-tan der lah kon-trah-van-syon

I have not got enough money. Can I pay at the police station?
Je n'ai pas assez d'argent Puis-je payer au commissariat de police?
jer nay pah ah-say dahr-jan. pweej pay-yay oh koh-mee-sah-ryah der poh-lees

Accidents and the Police

I am very sorry. I am a visitor
Je suis désolé Je suis de passage
jer swee day-soh-lay. jer swee der pah-sahj

I did not know about the speed limit
Je ne savais pas que la vitesse était limitée
jer ner sah-vay pah ker lah vee-tais ay-tay lee-mee-tay

I did not understand the sign
Je n'ai pas compris le panneau
jer nay pah kohm-pree ler pah-noh

I did not see the sign
Je n'ai pas vu le panneau
jer nay pah vew ler pah-noh

I did not see the bicycle
Je n'ai pas vu la bicyclette
jer nay pah vew lah bee-see-klait

I could not stop in time
Je n'ai pas pu m'arrêter à temps
jer nay pah pew mah-rai-tay ah tan

I have not had anything to drink
Je n'ai rien bu
jer nay ryern bew

I was only driving at 50 km/h
Je ne roulais qu'à 50 km/h
jer ner roo-lay kah san-kant kee-loh-maitr ah lerr

I was overtaking
J'étais en train de dépasser
jay-tay an trern der day-pah-say

Accidents and the Police

I was parking
J'étais en train de me garer
jay-tay an trern der mer gah-ray

That car was too close
La voiture me suivait de trop près
lah vwah-tewr mer swee-vay der troh prai

The brakes failed
Les freins ont lâché
lay frern zon lah-shay

The car number (license number) was...
Le numéro d'immatriculation était
ler new-may-roh dee-mah-tree-kew-lah-syon ay-tay...

The car skidded
La voiture a dérapé
lah vwah-tewr ah day-rah-pay

The car swerved
La voiture a fait un écart
lah vwah-tewr ah fai tan ay-kahr

The car turned right without signalling
La voiture a tourné à droite sans prévenir
lah vwah-tewr ah toor-nay ah drwaht san pray-ver-neer

The road was icy
La route était verglacée
lah root ay-tay vair-glah-say

The tyre burst
Le pneu a éclaté
ler pner ah ay-klah-tay

Car parts

accelerator
accélérateur
ahk-say-lay-rah-terr

aerial
antenne
an-tain

air filter
filtre à air
feeltr ah air

alternator
alternateur
ahl-tair-nah-terr

antifreeze
antigel
an-tee-jail

automatic
automatique
oh-toh-mah-teek

axle
essieu
ai-swee

battery
accus
ah-kew

bonnet
capot
kah-poh

boot
coffre
kohfr

brake fluid
lockheed
loh-keed

brakes
freins
frern

bulb
ampoule
an-pool

bumper
pare-chocs
pahr-shohk

carburettor
carburateur
kahr-bew-rah-terr

child seat
siège pour enfant
syaij poor an-fan

Car parts

choke
starter
stahr-tair

clutch
embrayage
an-brai-yaj

cylinder
cylindre
see-lerndr

disc brake
freins à disques
frern ah deesk

distributor
delco
dail-koh

door
portière
pohr-tyair

dynamo
dynamo
dee-nah-moh

electrical system
circuit électrique
seer-kwee ay-laik-treek

engine
moteur
moh-terr

exhaust system
échappement
ay-shahp-man

fan belt
courroie de ventilateur
koo-rwah der van-tee-lah-terr

foot pump
pompe à pied
pohmp ah pyay

fuel gauge
jauge d'essence
johj dai-sans

fuel pump
pompe d'alimentation
pohmp dah-lee-man-tah-syon

fuse
fusible
few-seebl

gear box
boîte de vitesses
bwaht der vee-tais

gear lever
levier de vitesses
lai-vyay der vee-tais

generator
génératrice
jay-nay-rah-trees

Car parts

hammer
marteau
mahr-toh

hand brake
frein à main
frern ah mern

hazard lights
feux de détresse
fer der day-trais

headlights
phares
fahr

heating system
chauffage
shoh-fahj

hood
capote
kah-poht

horn
klaxon
klahk-son

hose
tuyau
tew-yoh

ignition
allumage
ah-lew-mahj

ignition key
clef de contact
klay der kon-tahkt

indicator
clignotant
kleen-yoh-tan

jack
cric
kreek

lights
feux
fer

lock
dispositif antivol
dees-poh-see-teef an-tee-vohl

muffler
silencieux
see-lan-syer

oil filter
filtre à huile
feeltr ah weel

oil
huile
weel

oil pressure
pression d'huile
prai-syon dweel

Car parts

petrol
essence
ai-sans

points
vis platinées
vee plah-tee-nay

pump
pompe
pohmp

radiator
radiateur
rah-dyah-terr

rear view mirror
rétroviseur
ray-troh-vee-serr

reflectors
réflecteurs
ray-flaik-terr

reversing light
feux de recul
fer der rer-kewl

roof-rack
galerie
gah-ler-ree

screwdriver
tournevis
toorn-vee

seat belt
ceinture de sécurité
sern-tewr der say-kew-ree-tay

seat
siège
see-aij

shock absorber
amortisseur
ah-mohr-tee-serr

silencer
silencieux
see-lan-syer

socket set
prise
preez

spanner
clef anglaise
klay an-glay

spare part
pièce détachée
pyais day-tah-shay

spark plug
bougie
boo-jee

speedometer
compteur
kohmp-terr

Car parts

starter motor
démarreur
day-mah-rerr

steering
direction
dee-raik-syon

steering wheel
volant
voh-lan

stoplight
feu rouge
fer rooj

sun roof
toit ouvrant
twa toov-ran

suspension
suspension
sews-pan-syon

tools
outils
oo-tee

towbar
barre de remorquage
bahr der rer-mohr-kahj

transmission
transmission
trans-mee-syon

trunk
coffre
kohfr

tyre
pneu
pner

tyre pressure
pression des pneus
prai-syon day pner

warning light
voyant lumineux
voh-yan lew-mee-ner

water
eau
oh

wheel
roue
roo

windscreen
pare-brise
pahr-breez

wipers
essuie-glace
ais-wee-glahs

wrench
clef anglaise
klay an-glay

Road signs

passage interdit
no thoroughfare
pah-sahj ern-tair-dee

entrée interdite
no entry
an-tray ern-tair-deet

chemin privé
private road
sher-mern pree-vay

serrez à droite
keep to the right
sai-ray ah drwaht

déviation
diversion
day-vyah-syon

parking réservé aux résidents
parking for residents only
pahr-keeng ray-sair-vay oh ray-zee-dan

EATING OUT

Reservations

Should we reserve a table?
Faut-il réserver une table?
foh-teel ray-sair-vay ewn tahbl

Can I book a table for four at 8 o'clock?
Je voudrais réserver une table pour quatre pour huit heures
jer voo-dray ray-sair-vay ewn tahbl poor kahtr poor weet err

Can we have a table for four?
Une table pour quatre, s'il vous plaît
ewn tahbl poor kahtr, seel voo play

We would like a table — by the window
Nous voudrions une table — près de la fenêtre
noo voo-dryon ewn tahbl — prai der lah fer-naitr

— on the terrace
— sur la terrasse
— sewr lah tay-rahs

I am a vegetarian
Je suis végétarien
jer swee vay-jay-tah-ryern

Useful questions

Do you have a local speciality?
Avez-vous une spécialité régionale?
ah-vay voo zewn spay-syah-lee-tay ray-jyon-ahl

Useful questions

Do you have a set menu?
Avez-vous un menu à prix fixe?
ah-vay voo ern mer-new ah pree feeks

What do you recommend?
Que recommandez-vous?
ker rer-koh-man-day voo

What is the dish of the day?
Quel est le plat du jour?
kail ai ler plah dew joor

What is the soup of the day?
Quelle est la soupe du jour?
kail ai lah soop dew joor

What is this called?
Comment s'appelle ce plat?
koh-man sah-pail ser plah

What is this dish like?
Ce plat, qu'est-ce que c'est?
ser plah, kais ker sai

Is this good?
Est-ce que c'est bon?
ais ker sai bon

Which local wine do you recommend?
Quel vin de pays recommandez-vous?
kail vern der payy rer-koh-man-day voo

Are vegetables included?
Est-ce que les légumes sont inclus?
ais ker lay lay-gewm son tern-klew

Ordering your meal

Is the local wine good?
Est-ce que le vin de pays est bon?
ais ker ler vern der payy ai bon

Is this cheese very strong?
Ce fromage est-il très fort?
ser froh-mahj ai-teel trai fohr

How much is this?
C'est combien?
sai kohm-byern

Do you have yoghurt?
Avez-vous du yaourt?
ah-vay voo dew yah-oor

How do I eat this?
Comment mange-t-on cela?
koh-man manj-ton ser-lah

Ordering your meal

The menu, please
Le menu, s'il vous plaît
ler mer-new, seel voo play

Can we start with soup?
De la soupe pour commencer, s'il vous plaît
der lah soop poor koh-man-say, seel voo play

That is for me
C'est pour moi
sai poor mwah

Ordering your meal

Can we have some bread?
Du pain, s'il vous plaît
dew pern, seel voo play

Could we have some butter?
Du beurre, s'il vous plaît
dew berr, seel voo play

I will have salad
Je prendrai de la salade
jer pran-drai der lah sah-lahd

I will take that
Je prendrai ceci
jer pran-drai ser-see

I will take the set menu
Je prendrai le menu à prix fixe
jer pran-drai ler mer-new ah pree feeks

  I like my steak — rare
J'aime mon steack — saignant
  jaim mon staik — sai-nyan

            — medium rare
            — steack à point
            — staik ah pwan

            — very rare
            — steack bleu
            — staik bler

            — well done
            — steack bien cuit
            — staik byern kwee

Ordering drinks

Could we have some more bread please?
Encore du pain, s'il vous plaît
an-kohr dew pern, seel voo play

Can I see the menu again, please?
Repassez-moi le menu, s'il vous plaît
rer-pah-say mwah ler mer-new, seel voo play

Ordering drinks

The wine list, please
La carte des vins, s'il vous plaît
lah kahrt day vern, seel voo play

A bottle of house red wine, please
Une bouteille de la cuvée du patron, s'il vous plaît
ewn boo-tery der lah kew-vay dew pah-tron, seel voo play

A glass of dry white wine, please
Un verre de vin blanc, s'il vous plaît
ern vair der vern blan, seel voo play

Another bottle of red wine, please
Une autre bouteille de vin rouge, s'il vous plaît
ewn ohtr boo-tery der vern rooj, seel voo play

Another glass, please
Un autre verre, s'il vous plaît
ern ohtr vair, seel voo play

We will take the beaujolais
Nous prendrons le beaujolais
noo pran-dron ler boh-joh-lay

Ordering drinks

Two beers, please
Deux bières, s'il vous plaît
der byair, seel voo play

Some plain water, please
De l'eau du robinet, s'il vous plaît
der loh dew roh-bee-nay, seel voo play

Can we have some mineral water?
De l'eau minérale, s'il vous plaît
der loh mee-nay-rahl, seel voo play

Black coffee, please
Un café noir, s'il vous plaît
ern kah-fay nwahr, seel voo play

Coffee with milk, please
Un café au lait, s'il vous plaît
ern kah-fay oh lay, seel voo play

Paying the bill

What is the total?
Ça fait combien en tout?
sah fai kohm-byern an too

Do you accept traveller's cheques?
Acceptez-vous les chèques de voyage?
ahk-saip-tay voo lay shaik der vohy-ahj

I would like to pay with my credit card
Je voudrais payer avec ma carte de crédit
jer voo-dray pay-yay ah-vaik mah kahrt der kray-dee

Paying the bill

Is there any extra charge?
Y a-t-il un supplément?
ee-ah-teel ern sew-play-man

Is service included?
Est-ce que le service est compris?
ais ker ler sair-vees ai kohm-pree

Can I have a receipt?
Puis-je avoir un reçu?
pwee-jer ah-vwahr ern rer-sew

Can I have an itemised bill?
Puis-je avoir une facture détaillée?
pwee-jer ah-vwahr ewn fahk-tewr day-tah-yay

You have given me the wrong change
Vous vous êtes trompé en me rendant monnaie
voo voo zait trohm-pay an mer ran-dan moh-nay

This is not correct
C'est inexact
sai tee-naig-sahkt

This is not my bill
Ceci n'est pas ma facture
ser-see nai pah mah fahk-tewr

I do not have enough currency
Je n'ai pas assez de liquide
jer nay pah ah-say der lee-keed

I do not have enough money
Je n'ai pas assez d'argent
jer nay pah ah-say dahr-jan

Complaints and compliments

Complaints and compliments

Waiter! We have been waiting for a long time.
Garçon! Nous attendons depuis longtemps
gahr-sohn! noo zah-tan-don der-pwee lon-tan

This is cold
C'est froid
sai frwah

This is not what I ordered
Ce n'est pas ce que j'ai commandé
ser nai pah ser ker jay koh-man-day

Can I have the recipe?
Puis-je avoir la recette?
pwee-jer ah-vwahr lah rer-sait

This is excellent
C'est délicieux
sai day-lee-syer

The meal was excellent
Le repas était délicieux
ler rer-pah ay-tai day-lee-syer

Menu reader

abricots
ahb-ree-koh
apricots

ail
ah-ee
garlic

ananas
ah-nah-nah
pineapple

artichaut
ahr-tee-shoh
artichoke

asperge
ahs-pairj
asparagus

aubergine
oh-bair-jeen
aubergine

aubergines farcies
oh-bair-jeen fahr-see
stuffed aubergines

avocat
ah-voh-kah
avocado

bananes
bah-nahn
bananas

basilic
bah-see-leek
basil

beignets
bay-nyay
doughnuts

beignets
bain-yay
fritters

betterave
bait-rahv
beetroot

beurre
berr
butter

bifteck
beef-taik
beefsteak

blanquette de veau
blan-kait der voh
veal in white sauce

Menu reader

boeuf bourguignon
berf boor-gee-nyon
beef stewed in red wine

boeuf braisé
berf bray-zay
braised beef

boeuf en daube
berf an dohb
beef stew

bouillabaisse
boo-yah-bais
spicy fish soup with garlic

bouillon de boeuf
boo-yon der berf
beef broth

bouillon de poulet
boo-yon der poo-lay
chicken broth

calmar
kahl-mahr
squid

canard
kah-nahr
duck

canard à l'orange
kah-nahr ah loh-ranj
duck with orange

carottes
kah-roht
carrots

cassis
kah-see
blackcurrants

céleri
say-lai-reec
celery

cerfeuil
sair-fery
chervil

cerises
ser-reez
cherries

champignons
shan-pee-nyon
mushrooms

champignons à l'ail
shan-peen-yon ah lah-ee
mushrooms with garlic

champignons en sauce
shan-peen-yon an sohs
mushrooms in sauce

chicorée
shee-koh-ray
chicory

Menu reader

chou
shoo
cabbage

choucroute
shoo-kroot
sauerkraut

chou-fleur
shoo-fler
cauliflower

choux de Bruxelles
shoo der brew-sail
Brussels sprouts

ciboulette
see-boo-lait
chives

citron
see-tron
lemon

civet de lapin
see-vay der lah-pern
rabbit stew

compote de pommes
kohm-poht der pohm
apple compote

concombre
kon-kohmbr
cucumber

confiture
kon-fee-tewr
jam

coq au vin
kohk oh vern
coq au vin

cornichon
kohr-nee-shon
gherkin

côtelette d'agneau
koht-lait dahn-yoh
lamb cutlet

côtelette de porc
koht-lait der pohr
pork cutlet

côtelette de veau
koht-lait der voh
veal cutlet

côtelette grillée
koht-lait gree-yay
grilled cutlet

coulis de pommes
koo-lee der pohm
applesauce

courge
koorj
squash

Menu Reader

courgettes
koor-jait
courgettes

couscous
koos-koos
meat served with semolina,
vegetables and spicy sauce

crème anglaise
kraim an-glay
custard

crème caramel
kraim kah-rah-mail
caramel cream

cresson
krai-son
watercress

crêpes
kraip
thin pancakes

— à la confiture
— ah lah kon-fee-tewr-
— with jam

— au chocolat
— oh shoh-koh-lah-
— with chocolate

croque-monsieur
krohk-mer-syer
cheese and ham toasted
sandwich

cuisses de grenouilles
kwees der grer-nwee
frogs' legs

dattes
daht
dates

dessert
day-sair
pudding

dinde
dernd
turkey

échalottes
ay-shah-loht
shallots

en sauce
an sohs
in sauce

épinards
ay-pee-nahr
spinach

Menu reader

épinards
ay-pee-nahr
spinach

estragon
ais-trah-gon
tarragon

faisan
fay-san
pheasant

feuille de laurier
fery der loh-ryay
bayleaf

fèves
faiv
broad beans

filet de boeuf
fee-lay der berf
steak fillet

filet de colin
fee-lay der koh-lern
hake fillet

flan au fromage blanc
flan oh froh-mahj blan
cheese cake

fondue savoyarde
fon-dew sah-voh-yahrd
cheese fondue

fraises
fraiz
strawberries

fraises à la crème fraîche
fraiz ah lah kraim fraish
strawberries with cream

framboises
fran-bwahz
raspberries

frites
freet
French fries/chips

fruits à la crème fouettée
frwee zah lah kraim fwai-tay
fruit with whipped cream

gâteau
gah-toh
cake

gâteau aux amandes
gah-toh oh zah-mand
almond cake

gâteau de riz
gah-toh der ree
rice pudding

gâteau de Savoie
gah-toh der sah-vwah
sponge cake

Menu reader

gigot d'agneau
jee-goh dahn-yoh
roast leg of lamb

huîtres
weetr
oysters

glace
glahs
ice cream

jambon fumé
jan-bon few-may
cured ham

grenades
grer-nahd
pomegranates

jardinière de légumes
jahr-dee-nyair der lay-gewm
cubed vegetables

grillé/au feu de bois
gree-yay/oh fer der bwah
grilled/barbecued

jarret (d'agneau, etc.)
jah-ray (dahn-yoh)
shank (of lamb etc)

hachis parmentier
ahshee pahr-man-tyay
mince and mash au gratin

laitue
lay-tew
lettuce

haricots blancs
ah-ree-koh blan
baked beans

laitue
lay-tew
lettuce

haricots verts
ah-ree-koh vair
French beans

langouste
lan-goost
crayfish

homard
oh-mahr
lobster

langue
lang
tongue

huile
weel
oil

lapin farci
lah-pern fahr-see
stuffed rabbit

Menu reader

légumes
lay-gewm
vegetables

maïs
mah-ees
sweet corn

maquereau
mahk-roh
mackerel

maquereau mariné
mahk-roh mah-ree-nay
marinated mackerel

melon
mer-lon
melon

menthe
mant
mint

meringue au citron
may-rerng oh see-tron
lemon meringue

moules
mool
mussels

mousse au chocolat
moos oh shoh-koh-lah
chocolate mousse

moules frites
mool freet
mussels and French fries

moules marinières
mool mah-ree-nyair
mussels in wine and garlic

navet
nah-vay
turnip

oeuf à la coque
erf ah lah kohk
soft boiled egg

oeufs au bacon
er zoh bah-kon
eggs with bacon

oeufs au jambon
er zoh jan-bon
eggs with ham

oeufs au plat
er zoh plah
eggs sunny side up

oeufs brouillés
er brwee-yay
scrambled eggs

oie
wah
goose

Menu reader

oignons
wahn-yon
onions

olives
oh-leev
olives

oranges
oh-ranj
oranges

palourdes
pah-loord
clams

pamplemousse
panp-moos
grapefruit

panais
pah-nai
parsnip

pastèque
pahs-taik
watermelon

pâtes
paht
pasta

pâtes aux oeufs
paht oh zer
egg noodles

pêche
paish
peach

persil
pair-seel
parsley

petits pains
per-tee pern
bread rolls

petits pois
per-tee pwa
sweet peas

petits pois
per-tee pwah
peas

poire
pwahr
pear

poireaux
pwah-roh
leeks

poisson
pwah-son
fish

poisson mariné
pwah-son mah-ree-nay
marinated fish

Menu reader

poivron rouge
pwahv-ron rooj
red pepper

poivron vert
pwahv-ron vair
green pepper

pomme au four
pohm oh foor
roast apple

pommes
pohm
apples

**pommes de terre
dauphinoises**
pohm der tair doh-fee-nwahz
sliced potatoes baked with
cream and cheese

pommes rôties
ohm roh-tee
roast potatoes

potage aux champignons
poh-tahj oh shan-pee-nyon
cream of mushroom soup

**potage aux haricots
rouges**
poh-tahj oh zah-ree-koh rooj
kidney-bean soup

potage aux poireaux
poh-tahj oh pwah-roh
leek soup

potage aux pois
poh-tahj oh pwah
pea soup

potage aux tomates
poh-tahj oh toh-maht
tomato soup

potage de légumes
poh-tahj der lay-gewm
cream of vegetables soup

potage de poulet
poh-tahj der poo-lay
chicken soup

poulet frit/pané
poo-lay freet/pah-nay
fried/breaded chicken

poulet rôti
poo-lay roh-tee
baked/roasted chicken

prunes
prewn
plums

purée de pommees de terre
pew-ray der pohm der tair
mashed potatoes

Menu reader

radis
rah-dee
radishes

ragoût de boeuf
rah-goo der berf
beef stew

ragoût de poulet
rah-goo der poo-lay
chicken stew

raisin
rai-zern
grapes

reines-claude
rain-klohd
greengages

rillettes
reel-ait
potted meat

rognons en sauce
roh-nyon an sohs
stewed kidney

romarin
roh-mah-rern
rosemary

rôti de porc
roh-tee der pohr
pork roast

rouget
roo-jay
mullet

salade
sah-lahd
salad

salade composée
sah-lahd kohm-poh-say
mixed salad

salade de concombre
sah-lahd der kon-kohmbr
cucumber salad

salade de fruits
sah-lahd der frwee
fruit salad

salade de maïs
sah-lahd der mah-ees
corn salad

salade de pommes de terre
sah-lahd der pohm der tair
potato salad

salade de tomates
sah-lahd der toh-maht
tomato salad

salade russe
sah-lahd rews
Russian salad

Menu reader

sandwich au jambon
san-weesh oh jan-bon
ham sandwich

sandwich froid
san-weesh frwah
cold sandwich

sardines
sahr-deen
sardines

sauce à l'oignon
sohs ah loh-nyon
onion sauce

sauce au vin
sohs oh vern
wine sauce

sauce aux poivrons verts
sohs oh pwahv-ron vair
green pepper sauce

sauce tomate
sohs toh-maht
tomato sauce

saucisse
soh-sees
sausage

sauge
sohj
sage

scampi
skahm-pee
scampi

seiche
saish
cuttlefish

sole meunière
sohl mer-nyair
sole in butter with parsley

steack au poivre
staik oh pwahvr
pepper steak

steack frites
staik freet
steak and French fries

tarte
tahrt
pie

tarte aux pommes
tahrt oh pohm
apple tart

thon
ton
tuna

thym
tern
thyme

Drinks

tomates
toh-maht
tomatoes

tripes
treep
tripe

truite
trweet
trout

truite au beurre
trweet oh berr
fried trout

truite grillée
trweet gree-yay
grilled trout

viande
vee-and
meat

viande grillée
vee-and gree-yay
grilled meats

vinaigre
vee-naigr
vinegar

wiener schnitzel
ais-kah-lohp der voh pah-nay
escalope de veau panée

yaourt
yah-oor
yoghurt

Drinks

astis
ahs-tee
aniseed spirit

calvados
kahl-vah-doh
apple brandy

armagnac
ahr-mahn-yahk
armagnac

bière brune
byair brewn
stout

bière
byair
beer

bière en boîte
byair an bwaht
canned beer

Drinks

bière en canette
byair an kah-nait
bottled beer

cognac
kohn-yahk
brandy

café au lait
kah-fay oh lay
coffee with milk

café crème
kah-fay kraim
coffee with steamed milk

café glacé
kah-fay glah-say
iced coffee

café
kah-fay
coffee

café soluble
kah-fay soh-lewb
instant coffee

calvados
kahl-vah-doh
apple brandy

camomille
kah-moh-meel
camomile tea

champagne
shan-pah-nyer
champagne

kirsch
keersh
cherry brandy

cidre
seedr
cider

coca-cola
koh-kah-koh-lah
coke

café au lait
kah-fay oh lay
coffee with milk (breakfast)

café crème
kah-fay kraim
coffee with steamed milk

déca
day-kah
decaffeinated coffee

eau minérale
oh mee-nay-rahl
mineral water

café irlandais
kah-fay eer-lan-day
Irish coffee

Drinks

jus d'orange
jew doh-ranj
orange juice

jus de pomme
jew der pohm
apple juice

jus de raisin
jew der rai-zern
grape juice

kir
keer
blackcurrant liqueur

limonade
lee-moh-nahd
lemonade

liqueur
lee-kerr
liqueur

nectar d'abricot
naik-tahr dah-bree-koh
apricot juice

nectar de pêche
naik-tahr der paish
peach juice

orangeade
oh-ran-jahd
orange drink

rhum
ron
rum

sangria
sahn-gree-ah
sangria

Schweppes
shwaips
tonic water

express
aiks-prai
small black coffee

soda
soh-dah
soda

thé au lait
tay oh lay
tea with milk

thé citron
tay see-tron
lemon tea

un cognac
an koh-nyahk
a brandy

un verre de vin blanc
ern vair der vern blan
a glass of white wine

Drinks

un verre de vin rouge
ern vair der vern rooj
a glass of red wine

une bière
ewn byair
a large beer

vin rosé
vern roh-zay
rosé wine

whisky
wees-kee
whisky

OUT AND ABOUT

The weather

Isn't it a lovely day?
Belle journée, n'est-ce pas?
bail joor-nay, nais pah

Is it going to get any warmer?
Est-ce qu'il va faire plus chaud?
ais keel vah fair plew shoh

Is it going to stay like this?
Est-ce que ce temps va durer?
ais ker ser tan vah dew-ray

Is there going to be a thunderstorm?
Va-t-il y avoir un orage?
vah-teel ee ah-vwahr ern oh-rahj

It has stopped snowing
Il ne neige plus
eel ner naij plew

There is a cool breeze
Il y a un vent frais
eel yah ern van frai

What is the temperature?
Quelle est la température?
kail ai lah tan-pay-rah-tewr

Will the weather improve?
Est-ce que le temps va s'arranger?
ais ker ler tan vah sah-ran-jay

The weather

It is far too hot
Il fait beaucoup trop chaud
eel fai boh-koo troh shoh

It is foggy
Il y a du brouillard
eel yah dew brwee-yahr

It is going to be fine
Il va   faire beau
eel vah fair boh

It is going to be windy
Il va faire du vent
eel vah fair dew van

It is going to rain
Il va pleuvoir
eel vah pler-vwahr

It is going to snow
Il va neiger
eel vah nai-jay

It is raining again
Il pleut de nouveau
eel pler der noo-voh

It is very cold
Il fait très froid
eel fai trai frwah

It is very windy
Il y a beaucoup de vent
eel yah boh-koo der van

On the beach

Will the wind die down?
Est-ce que le vent va tomber?
ais-ker ler van vah tohm-bay

On the beach

Can you recommend a quiet beach?
Pouvez-vous nous recommander une plage tranquille?
poo-vay voo noo rer-koh-man-day ewn plahj tran-keel

Is it safe to swim here?
Peut-on se baigner ici sans danger?
per-ton ser bain-yay ee-see san dan-jay

Is the current strong?
Est-ce que le courant est fort?
ais kerler koo-ran ai fohr

Is the sea calm?
Est-ce que la mer est calme?
ais ker lah mair ai kahlm

Is the water warm?
Est-ce que l'eau est chaude?
ais ker loh ai shohd

Is there a lifeguard here?
Y a-t-il un maître nageur?
ee-ah-teel an maitr nah-jerr

Is this beach private?
Est-ce que la plage est privée?
ais ker lah plahj ai pree-vay

On the beach

When is — high tide?
A quelle heure est — la marée haute?
ah kail err ai — lah mah-ree oht

— low tide?
— la marée basse?
— lah mah-ree bahs

Can we change here?
Peut-on se changer ici?
per-ton ser shan-jay ee-see

Can I rent — a sailing boat?
Puis-je louer — un voilier?
pweej loo-ay — ern vwah-lyay

— a rowing boat?
— une barque?
— ewn bahrk

Is it possible — to go sailing?
Peut-on faire de la — de la voile?
per-ton fair — der lah vwahl

— to go surfing?
— du surf?
— dew sewrf

— to go water skiing?
— du ski nautique?
— dew skee noh-teek

— to go wind surfing?
— de la planche à voile?
— der lah plansh ah vwahl

Sport and recreation

Can we play — tennis?
Peut-on jouer — au tennis?
per-ton joo-ay — oh tay-nees

— golf?
— au golf?
— oh gohlf

— volleyball?
— au volley-ball?
— oh voh-lay-bohl

Can I rent the equipment?
Puis-je louer le matériel?
pweej loo-ay ler mah-tay-ryail

Can we go riding?
Peut-on monter à cheval?
per-ton mon-tay ah sher-vahl

Where can we fish?
Où peut-on faire de la pêche?
oo per-ton fair der lah paish

Do we need a permit?
Ai-je besoin d'un permis?
ai-jer ber-zwern dern pair-mee

Is there a heated swimming pool?
Y a-t-il une piscine chauffée?
ee-ah-teel ewn pee-seen shoh-fay

Entertainment

Is there — a disco?
Y a-t-il — une discothèque?
ee-ah-teel — ewn dees-koh-taik

> **— a good nightclub?**
> — une bonne boîte de nuit?
> *— ewn bohn bwaht der nwee*

> **— a theatre?**
> — un théâtre?
> *— ern tay-ahtr*

> **— a casino?**
> — un casino
> *— kah-see-noh*

Are there any films in English?
Y a-t-il des films en anglais?
ee-ah-teel day feelm zan an-glay

How much is it per person?
Combien coûte par parsonne?
kohm-byern koot pahr pair-sohn

Two stall tickets, please
Deux orchestres, s'il vous plaît
der-zohr-kaistr, seel voo play

Two tickets, please
Deux billets, s'il vous plaît
der bee-yay, seel voo play

Entertainment

How much is it to get in?
C'est combien pour l'entrée?
sai kohm-byern poor lan-tray

Is there a reduction for children?
Y a-t-il une réduction pour les enfants?
ee-ah-teel ewn ray-dewk-syon poor lay zan-fan

Sightseeing

Are there any — boat trips on the river?
Y a-t-il — des promenades en bateau sur la rivière?
ee-ah-teel — day prohm-nahd an bah-toh sewr lah ree-vyair

— guided tours of the castle?
— des visites guidées du château?
— day vee-seet gee-day dew shah-toh

— guided tours?
— des visites guidées?
— day vee-seet gee-day

What is the admission charge?
Combien coûte le billet?
kohm-byern koot ler bee-yay

What is there to see here?
Qu'y a-t-il à voir par ici?
kyah-teel ah vwahr pahr ee-see

Can we go up to the top?
Peut-on aller jusqu'en haut?
per-ton ah-lay jewsk an oh

Sightseeing

What time does the gallery open?
A quelle heure ouvre la galerie?
ah kail err oovr lah gah-lai-ree

Can I take photos?
Puis-je prendre des photos?
pweej prandr day foh-toh

Can I use flash?
Puis-je utiliser le flash?
pweej ew-tee-lee-zay ler flahsh

When is the bus tour?
A quelle heure est l'excursion en autocar?
ah kail err ai laiks-kewr-syon an oh-toh-kahr

How long does the tour take?
Combien de temps dure l'excursion?
kohm-byern der tan dewr laiks-kewr-syon

What is this building?
Cet édifice, qu'est-ce que c'est?
sait ay-dee-fees, kais ker sai

When was it built?
Quand a-t-il été construit?
kan tah-teel ay-tay kon-strwee

Is it open to the public?
Est-il ouvert au public?
ai-teel oo-vair oh pewb-leek

Can we go in?
Peut-on entrer?
per-ton an-tray

Sightseeing

Is there a guide book?
Avez-vous un guide?
ah-vay voo zern geed

Is there a tour of the cathedral?
Y a-t-il une visite de la cathédrale?
ee-ah-teel ewn vee-seet der lah kah-tay-drahl

Is there an English-speaking guide?
Y a-t-il un guide anglophone?
ee-ah-teel ern geed an-gloh-fohn

Is this the best view?
Est-ce le plus beau panorama?
ais ler plew boh pah-noh-rah-mah

Souvenirs

Where can I buy postcards?
Où puis-je acheter des cartes postales?
oo pweej ahsh-tay day kahrt pohs-tahl

Where can we buy souvenirs?
Où peut-on acheter des souvenirs?
oo per ton ahsh-tay day soo-ver-neer

Have you got an English guidebook?
Avez-vous un guide en anglais?
ah-vay voo zern geed an an-glay

Have you got any colour slides?
Avez-vous des diapositives en couleur?
ah-vay voo day dyah-poh-see-teev an koo-lerr

Going to church

How much does that cost?
C'est combien, s'il vous plaît?
sai kohm-byern, seel voo play

Have you got anything cheaper?
Avez-vous quelque chose de moins cher?
ah-vay voo kail-ker shohz der mwan shair

Going to church

Where is — the Catholic church?
   Où est — l'église catholique?
      oo ai — lay-gleez kah-toh-leek

         — the Baptist church?
         — l'église baptiste?
         — lay-gleez bahp-teest

         — the mosque?
         — la mosquée?
         — lah mohs-kay

         — the Protestant church?
         — le temple?
         — ler tanpl

         — the synagogue?
         — la synagogue?
         — lah seen-ah-gohg

What time is the service?
A quelle heure est la messe?
ah kail err ai lah mais

Going to church

I would like to see — a priest
Je voudrais voir — un prêtre
jer voo-dray vwahr — ern praitr

> **— a minister**
> — un pasteur
> *— ern pahs-terr*

> **— a rabbi**
> — un rabbin
> *— ern rah-bern*

SHOPPING

General phrases and requests

Can I have that one
Je voudrais celui-là
jer voo-dray ser-lwee-lah

No, the other one
Non, l'autre
non, lohtr

Can I have that one over there?
Je voudrais l'autre, là-bas
jer voo-dray lohtr, lah-bah

Can I have the other one
Je voudrais l'autre
jer voo-dray lohtr

Can I have a carrier bag?
Avez-vous un sac?
ah-vay voo zern sahk

Can I pay for air insurance?
Puis-je payer l'assurance pour un colis avion?
pweej pay-yay lah-sew-rans poor ern koh-lee ah-vyon

Can I see that umbrella?
Puis-je regarder ce parapluie?
pweej rer-gahr-day ser pah-rah-plwee

Can I use traveller's cheques?
Puis-je utiliser des chèques de voyage?
pweej ew-tee-lee-zay day shaik der voh-yahj

General phrases and requests

Can you deliver to my hotel?
Pouvez-vous le livrer à mon hôtel?
poo-vay voo ler leev-ray ah mon oh-tail

Have you got anything cheaper?
Avez-vous quelque chose de moins cher?
ah-vay voo kail-ker shohz der mwan shair

How much does that cost?
C'est combien, s'il vous plaît?
sai kohm-byern, seel voo play

How much is it per kilo?
C'est combien le kilo?
sai kohm-byern ler kee-loh

How much is it per metre?
C'est combien le mètre?
sai kohm-byern ler maitr

I am looking for a souvenir
Je cherche un souvenir
jer shairsh ern soov-neer

I do not like it
Cela ne me plaît pas
ser-lah ner mer plai pah

I like this one
Ceci me plaît
ser-see mer plai

I will take this one
Je vais prendre celui-ci
jer vai prandr ser-lwee-see

General phrases and requests

Is there a reduction for children?
Y a-t-il une réduction pour les enfants?
ee-ah-teel ewn ray-dewk-syon poor lay zan-fan

Please forward a receipt to this address
Envoyez un reçu à cette adresse, je vous prie
an-vwah-yay ern rer-sew ah sait ah-drais, jer voo pree

Please pack it for shipment
Emballez-le pour l'expédition, s'il vous plaît
an-bah-lay-ler poor laiks-pay-dee-syon, seel voo play

Please wrap it up for me
Emballez-le, je vous prie
an-bah-lay-ler, jer voo pree

There is no need to wrap it
Ce n'est pas la peine de l'emballer
ser nai pah lah pain der lan-bah-lay

We need to buy some food
Nous voulons acheter de la nourriture
noo voo-lon ahsh-tay der lah noo-ree-tewr

Where can I buy cassette tapes and compact discs?
Où puis-je trouver des cassettes et des disques laser?
oo pwee-jer troo-vay day kah-sait ay day deesk lah-zair

Where can I buy some clothes?
Où puis-je acheter des vêtements?
oo pweej ahsh-tay day vait-man

Where can I buy tapes for my camcorder?
Où puis-je trouver des cassettes pour mon caméscope?
oo pweej troo-vay day kah-sait poor mon kah-may-skohp

General phrases and requests

Where can I get my camcorder repaired?
Où puis-je faire réparer mon caméscope?
oo pweej fair ray-pah-ray mon kah-may-skohp

Will you send it by air freight?
Pouvez-vous l'expédier par avion?
poo-vay voo laiks-pay-dyay pahr ah-vyon

Where is the children's department?
Où est le rayon enfants?
oo ai ler rah-yon an-fan

Where is the food department?
Où est le rayon alimentation?
oo ai ler rah-yon ah-lee-man-tah-syon

Buying groceries

I would like — a kilo of potatoes
 Je voudrais — un kilo de pommes de terre
jer voo-dray — ern kee-loh der pohm der tair

> **— a bar of chocolate**
> — une tablette de chocolat
> *— ewn tah-blait der shoh-koh-lah*

> **— a litre of milk**
> — un litre de lait
> *— ern leetr der lay*

> **— two steaks**
> — deux biftecks
> *— der beef-taik*

Groceries

Can I have — some sugar, please?
Je voudrais — du sucre, s'il vous plaît
jer voo-dray — dew sewkr, seel voo play

> **— a bottle of wine, please?**
> — une bouteille de vin, s'il vous plaît
> *— ewn boo-tery der vern, seel voo play*

> **— 5 slices of ham, please?**
> — cinq tranches de jambon, s'il vous plaît
> *— sank transh der jan-bon, seel voo play*

> **— 100 g of ground coffee?**
> — cent grammes de café moulu, s'il vous plaît
> *— san grahm der kah-fay moo-lew, seel voo play*

> **— half a dozen eggs, please?**
> — six oeufs, s'il vous plaît
> *— see zer, seel voo play*

> **— half a kilo of butter, please?**
> — une livre de beurre, s'il vous plaît
> *— ewn leevr der berr, seel voo play*

Groceries

groceries
provisions
proh-vee-syon

baby food
aliments pour bébés
ah-lee-man poor bay-bay

biscuits
biscuits
bees-kwee

bread
pain
pern

Groceries

butter
beurre
berr

cheese
fromage
froh-mahj

coffee
café
kah-fay

cream
crème
kraim

eggs
oeufs
er

flour
farine
fah-reen

jam
confiture
kon-fee-tewr

margarine
margarine
mahr-gah-reen

milk
lait
lay

mustard
moutarde
moo-tahrd

oil
huile
weel

pepper
poivre
pwahvr

rice
riz
ree

salt
sel
sail

soup
soupe
soop

sugar
sucre
sewkr

tea
thé
tay

yoghurt
yaourt
yah-oor

Meat and fish

meat
viande
vee-and

beef
boeuf
berf

chicken
poulet
poo-lay

ham
jambon
jan-bon

lamb
agneau
ahn-yoh

liver
foie
fwah

kidneys
rognons
rohn-yon

pork
porc
pohr

veal
veau
voh

fish
poisson
pwah-son

cod
morue
moh-rew

herring
hareng
ah-raing

mussels
moules
mool

sole
sole
sohl

At the newsagent's

At the newsagent's

I would like — some postage stamps
Je voudrais — des timbres
jer voo-dray — day termbr

           — postcards
           — des cartes postales
           — day kahrt pohs-tahl

   I need — some adhesive tape
Il me faut — du scotch
eel mer foh — dew skohtsh

           — a bottle of ink
           — une bouteille d'encre
           — zewn boo-tery dankr

           — a pen
           — un stylo
           — zern stee-loh

           — a pencil
           — un crayon
           — zern kray-yon

           — some envelopes
           — des enveloppes
           — day zan-vai-lohp

           — some note paper
           — du papier à lettres
           — dew pah-pyay ah laitr

At the newsagent's

Do you have — English paperbacks?
Avez-vòus — des livres de poche anglais?
ah-vay voo — day leevr der pohsh an-glay

> **— a local map?**
> — une carte de la région?
> *— ewn kahrt der lah ray-jyon*

> **— street maps?**
> — des plans de ville?
> *— day plan der veel*

> **— a road map?**
> — une carte routière?
> *— zewn kahrt roo-tyair*

> **— coloured pencils?**
> — des crayons de couleur?
> *— day kray-yon der koo-lerr*

> **— felt pens?**
> — des stylos-feutre?
> *— day stee-loh fertr*

> **— drawing paper?**
> — du papier à dessin?
> *— dew pah-pyay ah dai-sern*

> **— English newspapers?**
> — des journaux anglais?
> *— day joor-noh zan-glay*

> **— English books?**
> — des livres anglais?
> *— day leevr zan-glay*

At the tobacconist's

At the tobacconist's

Do you have— cigarette papers?
 Avez-vous — du papier à cigarettes?
 ah-vay voo — dew pah-pyay ah see-gah-rait

> **— a box of matches?**
> — une boîte d'allumettes?
> *— ewn bwaht dah-lew-mait*

> **— a cigar?**
> — un cigare?
> *— ern see-gahr*

> **— a cigarette lighter?**
> — un briquet?
> *— ern bree-kay*

> **— a pipe?**
> — une pipe?
> *— ewn peep*

> **— a gas (butane) refill?**
> — une cartouche de gaz?
> *— ewn kahr-toosh der gahz*

> **— a pouch of pipe tobacco?**
> — un paquet de tabac à pipe?
> *— ern pah-kay der tah-bahk ah peep*

> **— some pipe cleaners?**
> — des cure-pipes?
> *— day kewr-peep*

At the chemist's

A packet of...please
Un paquet de   s'il vous plaît
ern pah-kay der... seel voo play

A packet of...please, with filter tips
Un paquet de   s'il vous plaît, à bout filtre
ern pah-kay der... seel voo play, ah boo feeltr

A packet of...please, without filters
Un paquet de   s'il vous plaît, sans filtre
ern pah-kay der... seel voo play, san feeltr

Have you got any — English brands?
Avez-vous — des cigarettes anglaises?
ah-vay voo — day see-gah-rait an-glaiz

— American brands?
— des cigarettes américaines?
— day see-gah-rait ah-may-ree-kain

— rolling tobacco?
— du tabac á cigarettes?
— dew tah-bahk ah see-gaa-rait

At the chemist's

I need some high-protection suntan cream
Je veux une crème solaire pour peau délicate
jer ver ewn kraim soh-lair poor poh day-lee-kaht

Do you sell sunglasses?
Vendez-vous des lunettes de soleil?
van-day voo day lew-nait der soh-lery

At the chemist's

Can you give me something for — insect bites?
Avez-vous quelque chose pour — les piqûres d'insectes?
ah-vay voo kail-ker shohz poor — lay pee-kewr dern-saikt

> **— an upset stomach?**
> — mal à l'estomac?
> *— mahl ah lais-toh-mah*

> **— a cold?**
> — un rhume?
> *— ern rewm*

> **— a cough?**
> — une toux?
> *— ewn too*

> **— a headache?**
> — les maux de tête?
> *— lay moh der tait*

> **— a sore throat?**
> —un mal de gorge?
> *— ern mahl der gohrj*

> **— hay fever?**
> — rhume des foins?
> *— rewm day fwern*

> **— toothache?**
> — mal de dents?
> *— mahl der dan*

> **— sunburn?**
> — coup de soleil?
> *— koo der soh-lery*

Medicines and toiletries

Do I need a prescription?
Ai-je besoin d'une ordonnance?
ay-jer ber-zwern dewn ohr-doh-nans

How many do I take?
Combien de cachets dois-je prendre?
kohm-byern der kah-shay dwah-jer prandr

How often do I take them?
Tous les combien?
too lay kohm-byern

Are they safe for children to take?
Est-ce qu'ils conviennent aux enfants?
ais keel kon-vyain oh zan-fan

Medicines and toiletries

aftershave
aftershave
ahf-tair-shayv

antihistamine
antihistamine
an-tees-tah-meen

antiseptic
antiseptique
an-tee-saip-teek

aspirin
aspirine
ahs-pee-reen

band-aid
pansement adhésif
pans-man ahd-ay-zeef

bandage
pansement
pans-man

bath salt
sels de bain
sail der bern

bubble bath
bain mousseux
bern moo-ser

Medicines and toiletries

cleansing milk
lait démaquillant
lay day-mah-kee-yan

contraceptive
préservatif
pray-sair-vah-teef

cotton wool
coton hydrophile
koh-ton eed-roh-feel

deodorant
déodorant
day-oh-doh-ran

disinfectant
désinfectant
day-zern-faik-tan

eau de Cologne
eau de Cologne
oh der koh-lohn

eye shadow
fard à paupières
fahr dah poh-pyair

hair spray
laque
lahk

hand cream
crème pour les mains
kraim poor lay mern

insect repellent
insectifuge
an-saik-tee-fewj

kleenex
kleenex
klee-naiks

laxative
laxatif
lahk-sah-teef

lipstick
rouge à lèvres
rooj ah laivr

mascara
mascara
mahs-kah-rah

mouthwash
bain de bouche
bern der boosh

nail file
lime à ongles
leem ah ongl

nail varnish remover
dissolvant
dee-sohl-van

nail varnish
vernis à ongles
vair-nee ah ongl

Shopping for clothes

perfume
parfum
pahr-fern

powder
poudre
poodr

razor blades
lames de rasoir
lahm der rah-zwahr

sanitary towels
serviettes hygiéniques
sair-vyait ee-jay-neek

shampoo
shampooing
shahm-poo-eeng

shaving cream
crème à raser
kraim ah rah-zay

skin moisturiser
crème hydratante
kraim eed-rah-tant

soap
savon
sah-von

suntan oil
crème solaire
kraim soh-lair

talc
talc
tahlk

toilet water
eau de toilette
oh der twah-lait

toothpaste
dentifrice
dan-tee-frees

Shopping for clothes

I am just looking, thank you
Je ne fais que regarder, merci
jer ner fai ker rer-gahr-day, mair-see

I like that one there
J'aime bien celui-là
jaim byern ser-lwee-lah

Shopping for clothes

I like the one in the window
J'aime bien celui qui est en vitrine
jaim byern ser-lwee kee ai an vee-treen

I like this one
J'aime bien celui-ci
jaim byern ser-lwee-see

I like it
Il me plaît
eel mer plai

I do not like it
Il ne me plaît pas
eel ner mer plai pah

I will take it
Je le prends
jer ler pran

Can I change it if it does not fit?
Puis-je le rapporter s'il ne me va pas?
pweej ler rah-pohr-tay seel ner mer vah pah

Can you please measure me?
Pouvez-vous prendre mes mesures, s'il vous plaît?
poo-vay voo prandr may mer-sewr, seel voo play

Have you got a larger size?
Avez-vous une taille plus grande?
ah-vay voo ewn tah-ee plew grand

Have you got this in other colours?
Avez-vous ceci dans une autre teinte?
ah-vay voo ser-see dan zewn ohtr ternt

Shopping for clothes

I take a large shoe size
Je chausse grand
jer shohs gran

I take continental size... 43
Je chausse du   43
jer shohs dew... kah-rant trwah

I would like this suit
Je voudrais ce complet
jer voo-dray ser kohm-play

I would like one with a zip
J'en voudrais un avec une fermeture éclair
jan voo-dray ern ah-vaik ewn fairm-tewr ay-klair

I would like this hat
J'en voudrais ce chapeau
jan voo-dray ser shah-poh

I would like a smaller size
J'en voudrais une taille plus petite
jan voo-dray ewn tah-ee plew per-teet

Where are the changing (dressing) rooms?
Où sont les cabines d'essayage?
oo son lay kah-been dai-say-yahj

Where can I try it on?
Où puis-je l'essayer?
oo pweej lai-say-yay

Is it too long?
Est-ce trop long?
ais troh lon

Shopping for clothes

Is it too short?
Est-ce trop court?
ais troh koor

Is there a full-length mirror?
Y a-t-il un grand miroir?
ee-ah-teel ern gran meer-wahr

Is this all you have?
Est-ce tout ce que vous avez?
ais toos ker voo zah-vay

It does not fit
Il ne me va pas
eel ner mer vah pah

It does not suit me
Il ne me convient pas
eel ner mer kon-vyern pah

May I see it in daylight?
Puis-je le regarder à la lumière du jour?
pwee-jer ler rer-gahr-day ah lah lew-myair dew joor

Is it drip-dry?
Faut-il le repasser?
foh-teel ler rer-pah-say

Is it dry-clean only?
Faut-il le nettoyer à sec seulement?
foh-teel ler nai-twah-yay ah saik serl-man

Is it machine washable?
Est-ce lavable à la machine?
ais lah-vahbl ah lah mah-sheen

Clothes and accessories

What is it made of?
C'est en quel tissu?
sai tan kail tee-sew

Will it shrink?
Est-ce que ça rétrécit?
ais ker sah ray-tray-see

Clothes and accessories

acrylic
acrylique
ah-kree-leek

bracelet
bracelet
brahs-lay

belt
ceinture
sern-tewr

blouse
chemisier
sher-mee-zyay

bra
soutien-gorge
soo-tyern gohrj

brooch
broche
brohsh

button
bouton
boo-ton

cardigan
gilet
jee-lay

coat
manteau
man-toh

corduroy
velours côtelé
ver-loor koht-lay

denim
denim
der-neem

dress
robe
rohb

Clothes and accessories

dungarees
salopette
sah-loh-pait

earrings
boucles d'oreille
bookl doh-tray

fur
fourrure
foo-rewr

gloves
gants
gan

handbag
sac à main
sahk ah mern

handkerchief
mouchoir
moo-shwahr

hat
chapeau
shah-poh

jacket
veste
vaist

jeans
jean
djeen

jersey
tricot
tree-koh

lace
dentelle
dan-tail

leather
cuir
kweer

linen
toile de lin
twahl der lern

necklace
collier
koh-lyay

night-dress
chemise de nuit.
sher-meez der nwee

nylon
nylon
nee-lon

panties
slip
sleep

pendant
pendentif
pan-dan-teef

Clothes and accessories

petticoat
jupon
jew-pon

polyester
polyester
pohl-yais-tair

poplin
popeline
pohp-leen

pullover
pull-over
pewl-oh-vair

purse
porte-monnaie
pohrt moh-nai

pyjamas
pyjama
pee-jah-mah

raincoat
imperméable
ern-pair-may-ahbl

rayon
rayonne
ray-ohn

ring
bague
bahg

sandals
sandales
san-dahl

scarf
écharpe
ay-shahrp

shirt
chemise
sher-meez

shorts
short
shohrt

silk
soie
swah

skirt
jupe
jewp

slip
combinaison
kohm-bee-nay-son

socks
chaussettes
shoh-sait

stockings
bas
bah

Clothes and accessories

suede
daim
derm

suit (men's)
complet
kohm-plai

suit (women's)
tailleur
tah-yerr

sweater
chandail
shan-dah-ee

swimming trunks
maillot de bain
mah-yoh der bern

swimsuit
costume de bain
kohs-tewm der bern

t-shirt
T-shirt
tee-shairt

tie
cravate
krah-vaht

tights
collants
koh-lan

towel
serviette
sair-vyait

trousers
pantalon
pan-tah-lon

umbrella
parapluie
pah-rah-plwee

underpants
slip
sleep

velvet
velours
ver-loor

vest
maillot de corps
mah-yoh der kohr

watch
montre
montr

wool
laine
lain

zip
fermeture éclair
fairm-tewr ay-klair

Photography

Can you develop this film, please?
Pouvez-vous développer cette pellicule, s'il vous plaît?
poo-vay voo dayv-loh-pay sait pay-lee-kewl, seel voo play

I would like this photo enlarged
Je voudrais un agrandissement de cette photo
jer voo-dray zern ah-gran-dees-man der sait foh-toh

I would like two prints of this one
Je voudrais deux copies de cette photo
jer voo-dray der koh-pee der sait foh-toh

When will the photos be ready?
Quand est-ce que les photos seront prêtes?
kan ais ker lay foh-toh ser-ron prait

I need a film for — this camera
Je voudrais une pellicule pour — cet appareil
jer voo-dray zewn pay-lee-kewl poor — sait ah-pah-rery

— this camcorder
— ce caméscope
— ser kah-may-skohp

— this cine camera
— cette caméra
— sait kah-may-rah

— this video camera
— cette caméra vidéo
— sait kah-may-rah vee-dyoh

Photography

I want a black and white film
Je veux une pellicule noir et blanc
jer ver ewn pay-lee-kewl nwahr ay blan

I want batteries for the flash
Je veux des piles pour le flash
jer ver day peel poor ler flahsh

I want a colour slide film
Je veux une pellicule couleur pour diapositives
jer ver zewn pay-lee-kewl koo-lerr poor dyah-poh-see-teev

I want a colour print film
Je veux une pellicule couleur
jer ver zewn pay-lee-kewl koo-lerr

Camera repairs

I am having trouble with my camera
J'ai des problèmes avec mon appareil
jay day proh-blaim ah-vaik moh nah-pah-rery

There is something wrong with my camera
Mon appareil ne marche plus
moh nah-pah-rery ner mahrsh plew

This is broken
C'est cassé
sai kah-say

Where can I get my camera repaired?
Où puis-je faire réparer mon appareil?
oo pweej fair ray-pah-ray moh nah-pah-rery

Camera parts

Have you got a spare part for this?
Avez-vous une pièce de rechange pour ceci?
ah-vay voo zewn pyais der rer-shanj poor ser-see

The film is jammed
La pellicule est coincée
lah pay-lee-kewl ai kwern-say

Camera parts

accessory
accessoire
ahk-sai-swahr

blue filter
filtre bleu
feeltr bler

cassette
cassette
kah-sait

cartridge
cartouche
kahr-toosh

camcorder
caméscope
kah-may-skohp

cine camera
caméra
kah-may-rah

distance
distance
dees-tans

enlargement
agrandissement
ah-gran-dees-man

exposure
pose
pohz

exposure meter
posemètre
pohz-maitr

flash
flash
flahsh

flash bulb
ampoule de flash
an-pool der flahsh

Camera parts

flash cube
cube de flash
kewb der flahsh

focal distance
distance focale
dees-tans foh-kahl

focus
mise au point
meez oh pwan

in focus
net
nay

out of focus
flou
floo

image
image
ee-mahj

lens
objectif
ohb-jaik-teef

lens cover
bouchon d'objectif
boo-shon dohb-jaik-teef

over exposed
surexposé
sewr-aiks-poh-zay

picture
photo
foh-toh

projector
projecteur
proh-jaik-terr

print
épreuve
ay-prerv

negative
négatif
nay-gah-teef

red filter
filtre rouge
feeltr rooj

reel
bobine
boh-been

shade
nuance
new-ans

slide
diapositive
dyah-poh-zee-teef

shutter
obturateur
ohb-tew-rah-terr

shutter speed
vitesse d'obturateur
vee-tais dohb-tew-rah-terr

under exposed
sous-exposé
soo-zaiks-poh-zay

transparency
transparent
trans-pah-ran

viewfinder
viseur
vee-zerr

tripod
tripode
tree-pohd

wide angle lens
objectif grand angle
ohb-jaik-teef gran tangl

At the hairdresser's

I would like to make an appointment
Je voudrais prendre rendez-vous
jer voo-dray prandr ran-day-voo

I want a haircut
Je veux me faire couper les cheveux
jer ver mer fair koo-pay lay sher-ver

Please cut my hair short
Coupez mes cheveux court, s'il vous plaît
koo-pay may sher-ver koor, seel voo play

Please cut my hair in a fringe
Coupez mes cheveux avec une frange
koo-pay may sher-ver ah-vaik ewn franjr

Take a little more off the back
Dégagez un peu plus à l'arrière
day-gah-jay ern per plews ah lah-ryair

At the hairdresser's

I would like — a trim
 Je voudrais — une coupe d'entretien
jer voo-dray — ewn koop dantr-tyern

               — a conditioner
               — du baume démêlant
               — dew bohm day-mai-lan

               — a perm
               — une permanente
               — ewn pair-mah-nant

               — my hair streaked
               — des mèches
               — day maish

               — a blow-dry
               — un brushing
               — ern broo-sheeng

               — hair spray
               — de la laque
               — der lah lahk

               — my hair dyed
               — me faire teindre
               — mer fair terndr

               — shampoo and cut
               — shampooing et coupe
               — shahm-pweeng ay koop

               — shampoo and set
               — shampooing et mise en plis
               — shahm pweeng ay mee zan plee

That is fine, thank you
C'est parfait, merci
sai pahr-fai, mair-see

Not too much off
Pas trop
pah troh

The dryer is too hot
Le séchoir est trop chaud
ler say-shwahr ai troh shoh

The water is too hot
L'eau est trop chaude
loh ai troh shohd

Laundry

Is there a launderette nearby?
Y a-t-il une laverie automatique près d'ici?
ee-ah-teel ewn lahv-ree oh-toh-mah-teek prai dee-see

Can you clean this skirt?
Pouvez-vous laver cette jupe?
poo-vay voo lah-vay sait jewp

Can you clean and press these shirts?
Pouvez-vous laver et repasser ces chemises?
poo-vay voo lah-vay ay rer-pah-say say sher-meez

Can you wash these clothes?
Pouvez-vous laver ces vêtements?
poo-vay voo lah-vay say vait-man

Laundry

This stain is — oil
Cette tache est — de l'huile
  sait tahsh ai — der lweel

                    — blood
                    — du sang
                    — dew san

                    — coffee
                    — du café
                    — dew kah-fay

                    — ink
                    — de l'encre
                    — der lankr

This fabric is — delicate
  Ce tissu est — fin
ser tee-sew ai — fern

                    — damaged
                    — endommagé
                    — ai tan-doh-mah-jay

                    — torn
                    — déchiré
                    — day-shee-ray

Can you do it quickly?
Pouvez-vous le faire rapidement?
poo-vay voo ler fair rah-peed-man

When should I come back?
Quand dois-je revenir?
kan dwah-jer rerv-neer

General repairs

When will my things be ready?
Quand puis-je passer prendre mes vêtements?
kan pwee-jer pah-say prandr may vait-man

How does the machine work?
Comment marche cette machine?
koh-man mahrsh sait mah-sheen

How long will it take?
Il y en a pour combien de temps?
eel yan ah poor kohm-byern der tan

I have lost my dry cleaning ticket
J'ai perdu mon coupon de nettoyage à sec
jay pair-dew mon koo-pon der nai-twah-yahj ah saik

General repairs

Can you repair it?
Pouvez-vous le réparer?
poo-vay voo ler ray-pah-ray

Can you repair them?
Pouvez-vous les réparer?
poo-vay voo lay ray-pah-ray

Would you have a look at this please?
Pourriez-vous y jeter un coup d'oeil, s'il vous plaît?
poo-ryay voo zee jer-tay an koo dery, seel voo play

Here is the guarantee
Voici la garantie
vwah-see lah gah-ran-tee

General repairs

I need new heels on these shoes
Ces chaussures ont besoin de talons neufs
say shoh-sewr on ber-zwern der tah-lon nerf

I need them in a hurry
J'en ai besoin aussitôt que possible
john ay ber-zwern oh-see-toh ker poh-seebl

I will come back later
Je reviens plus tard
jer rer-vyern plew tahr

I will come back in an hour
Je reviens dans une heure
jer rer-vyern dan zewn err

Please send it to this address
Expédiez-le à cette adresse, s'il vous plaît
aiks-pay-dyay ler ah sait ah-drais, seel voo play

At the Post Office

Can I have a telegram form, please?
Donnez-moi un formulaire de télégramme, s'il vous plaît?
doh-nay mwah ern fohr-mew-lair der tay-lay-grahm, seel voo play

Can I have six stamps for postcards to Britain?
Donnez-moi six timbres pour cartes postales pour la Grande-Bretagne
doh-nay mwah see termbr poor kahrt pohs-tahl poor lah grand-brer-tahn

At the Post Office

How much is a letter to — Britain?
C'est combien pour une lettre pour — la Grande-Bretagne?
say kohm-byern poor ewn laitr poor — la grand-brer-tahn

— America?
— les États-Unis?
— *lays-ayta-ewni*

12 stamps, please
douze timbres, s'il vous plaît
dooz termbr, seel voo play

I need to send this by courier
Je voudrais envoyer ceci par coursier
jer voo-dray an-vwah-yay ser-see pahr koor-syay

I want to send a telegram
Je voudrais envoyer un télégramme
jer voo-dray an-vwah-yay ern tay-lay-grahm

I want to send this by registered mail
Je voudrais envoyer ceci en recommandé
jer voo-dray an-vwah-yay ser-see an rer-koh-man-day

I want to send this parcel
Je voudrais expédier ce colis
jer voo-dray aiks-pay-dyay ser koh-lee

When will it arrive?
Quand arrivera-t-il à destination?
kan tah-reev-rah teel ah days-tee-nah-syon

Can I use my credit card?
Puis-je utiliser ma carte de crédit?
pweej ew-tee-lee-say mah kahrt der kray-dee

Using the telephone

Using the telephone

Can I use the telephone, please?
Puis-je me servir du téléphone, s'il vous plaît?
pweej mer sair-veer dew tay-lay-fohn

I must make a phone call to Britain
Je voudrais téléphoner en Grande-Bretagne
jer voo-dray tay-lay-foh-nay an grand-brer-tahn

I need to make a phone call
Je veux téléphoner
jer ver tay-lay-foh-nay

How much is it to phone to Paris?
C'est combien pour téléphoner à Paris?
sai kohm-byern poor tay-lay-foh-nay ah pah-ree

I would like to make a reversed charge (collect) call
Je voudrais téléphoner en PCV
jer voo-dray tay-lay-foh-nay an pay-say-vay

The number I need is...
Le numéro est le
ler new-may-roh ai ler...

What is the code for — Britain?
Quel est l'indicatif pour — la Grande-Bretagne?
kail ai lern-dee-kah-teef poor — lah grand-brer-tahn

— America?
— les Ètats-Unis?
— lays-ayta-ewni

Using the telephone

Please, call me back
Rappelez-moi, s'il vous plaît
rah-play mwah, seel voo play

I am sorry. We were cut off
Je suis désolé On nous a coupés
jer swee day-soh-lay. on noo zah koo-pay

J'essaie d'obtenir votre communication
jai-say dohb-ter-neer vohtr koh-mew-nee-kah-syon
I am trying to connect you

Je ne peux pas obtenir ce numéro
jer ner per pah zohb-ter-neer ser new-may-roh
I cannot obtain this number

Je vous passe Monsieur Brown
jer voo pahs mer-syer Broon
I am putting you through to Mr Brown

La ligne est occupée
lah leen ai toh-kew-pay
The line is engaged (busy)

Le numéro est en dérangement
ler new-may-roh ai an day-ranj-man
The number is out of order

Allez-y, vous êtes en ligne
ah-lay-zee, voo zait an leen
Please go ahead

Changing money

Changing money

Can I change these traveller's cheques?
Puis-je changer ces chèques de voyage?
pweej shan-jay say shaik der voh-yahj

Can I change these notes (bills)?
Puis-je changer ces billets?
pweej shan-jay say bee-yay

Can I contact my bank to arrange for a transfer?
Puis-je contacter ma banque pour organiser un virement?
pweej kon-tahk-tay mah bank poor ohr-gah-nee-zay ern veer-man

Has my cash arrived?
Est-ce que mes fonds sont arrivés?
ais-ker may fon son tah-ree-vay

Here is my passport
Voici mon passeport
vwah-see mon pahs-pohr

I would like to cash a cheque with my Eurocheque card
Je voudrais encaisser un chèque avec ma carte Eurochèque
jer voo-dray an-kai-say ern shaik ah-vaik mah kahrt er-roh-shaik

I would like to obtain a cash advance with my credit card
Je voudrais une avance en liquide sur ma carte de crédit
jer voo-dray ewn ah-vans an lee-keed sewr mah kahrt der kray-dee

Changing money

This is the name and address of my bank
Voici le nom et l'adresse de ma banque
vwah-see ler nohm ay lah-drais der mah bank

What is the rate for — sterling?
Quel est le taux de change pour — la livre sterling?
kail ai ler toh der shanj poor — lah leevr stair-leeng

— American dollars?
— le dollar US?
— ler doh-lahr ew ais

What is the rate of exchange?
Quel est le taux de change?
kail ai ler toh der shanj

What is your commission?
Quelle est votre commission?
kail ai vohtr koh-mee-syon

HEALTH

What's wrong?

Can I see a doctor?
Puis-je voir un médecin?
pwee-jer vwahr an mayd-sern

I need a doctor
Je veux voir un médecin
jer ver vwahr an mayd-sern

He has been badly injured
Il a été grièvement blessé
eel ah ay-tay gree-aiv-man blay-say

He has burnt himself
Il s'est brûlé
eel sai brew-lay

He has dislocated his shoulder
Il s'est démis l'épaule
eel sai day-mee lay-pohl

He is hurt
Il s'est fait mal
eel sai fai mahl

He is unconscious
Il a perdu connaissance
eel ah pair-dew koh-nai-sans

She has a temperature
Elle a de la fièvre
ail ah der lah fyaivr

What's wrong

She has been bitten
Elle a été mordue
ail ah ay-tay mohr-dew

She has sprained her ankle
Elle s'est tordu la cheville
ail sai tohr-dew lah sher-vee

My son has cut himself
Mon fils s'est coupé
mon fees sai koo-pay

My arm is broken
Mon bras est cassé
mon brah ai kah-say

I am badly sunburnt
J'ai attrapé un mauvais coup de soleil
jay ah-trah-pay ern moh-vai koo der soh-lery

I am ill
Je suis malade
jer swee mah-lahd

I am constipated
Je suis constipé
jer swee kon-stee-pay

I am a diabetic
Je suis diabétique
jer swee dyah-bay-teek

I am allergic to penicillin
Je suis allergique à la pénicilline
jer swee zah-lair-jeek ah lah pay-nee-see-leen

What's wrong

I have — a headache
  J'ai — à la tête
  jay — ah lah tait

        — a pain here
        — mal là
        — mahl lah

        — a rash here
        — une éruption là
        — ewn ay-rewp-syon lah

        — sunstroke
        — une insolation
        — ewn ern-soh-lah-syon

        — been stung
        — été piqué
        — ay-tay pee-kay

        — a sore throat
        — mal à la gorge
        — mahl ah lah gohrj

        — an earache
        — mal aux oreilles
        — oh zoh-rery

        — cramp
        — une crampe
        — ewn krahmp

        — diarrhoea
        — la diarrhée
        — lah dyah-ray

What's wrong?

I have been sick
J'ai vomi
jay voh-mee

   I have — hurt my arm
  Je me suis — fait mal au bras
jer mer swee — fai mahl oh brah

      — hurt my leg
      — fait mal à la jambe
      — fai mahl ah lah janb

      — pulled a muscle
      — claqué un muscle
      — klah-kay ern mewskl

      — cut myself
      — coupé
      — koo-pay

  It is — inflamed here
 C'est— enflammé là
 say — tan-flah-may lah

      — painful to walk
      — douloureux de marcher
      — doo-loo-rer der mahr-shay

      — painful to breathe
      — douloureux de respirer
      — doo-loo-rer der rers-pee-ray

      — painful to swallow
      — douloureux d'avaler
      — doo-loo-rers dah-vah-lay

What's wrong?

I feel dizzy
J'ai des étourdissements
jay day zay-toor-dees-man

I feel faint
Je me sens faible
jer mer san faibl

I feel nauseous
J'ai la nausée
jay lah noh-say

I fell
Je suis tombé
jer swee tohm-bay

I cannot sleep
Je n'arrive pas à dormir
jer nah-reev pah ah dohr-meer

I think I have food poisoning
Je crois que j'ai une intoxication alimentaire
jer krwah ker jay ewn ern-tohk-see-kah-syon ah-lee-man-tair

My stomach is upset
J'ai mal à l'estomac
jay mahl ah lais-toh-mah

My tongue is coated
J'ai la langue chargée
jay lah lan-g shahr-jay

There is a swelling here
C'est enflé là
sai tan-flay lah

What's wrong?

I need some antibiotics
J'ai besoin d'antibiotiques
jay ber-zwan dan-tee-byoh-teek

I suffer from high blood pressure
Je fais de l'hypertension
jer fai der lee-pair-tan-syon

I am taking these drugs
Je prends ces médicaments
jer pran say may-dee-kah-man

Can you give me a prescription for them?
Pouvez-vous me donner une ordonnance pour ces
médicaments?
*poo-vay voo mer doh-nay ewn ohr-doh-nans poor say may-
dee-kah-man*

I am on the pill
Je prends la pilule
jer pran lah pee-lewl

I am pregnant
Je suis enceinte
jer swee zan-cernt

My blood group is...
Mon groupe sanguin est
mon groop san-gwern ai...

I do not know my blood group
Je ne sais pas quel est mon groupe sanguin
jer ner say pah kail ai mon groop san-gwern

At the hospital

Do I have to go into hospital?
Sera-t-il nécessaire de m'hospitaliser?
ser-ra-teel nay-say-sair der mohs-pee-tah-lee-zay

Do I need an operation?
Est-ce qu'il faudra m'opérer?
ais-keel foh-drah moh-pay-ray

Here is my E111 form
Voici mon formulaire E111
vwah-see mon fohr-mew-lair er san-tonz

How do I get reimbursed?
Comment serai-je remboursé?
koh-man ser-raij ran-boor-say

Must I stay in bed?
Dois-je garder le lit?
dwah-jer gahr-day ler lee

When will I be able to travel?
Quand serai-je en état de voyager?
kan ser-raij an ay-tah der voh-yah-jay

Will I be able to go out tomorrow?
Pourrai-je sortir demain?
poo-raij sohr-teer der-mern

Parts of the body

ankle
cheville
sher-vee

arm
bras
brah

back
dos
doh

bone
os
oh

breast
sein
sern

cheek
joue
joo

chest
poitrine
pwah-treen

ear
oreille
oh-rery

elbow
coude
kood

eye
oeil (pl yeux)
ery (yer)

face
visage
vee-sahj

finger
doigt
dwah

foot
pied
pyay

hand
main
mern

heart
coeur
kerr

kidney
rein
rern

Parts of the body

knee
genou
jer-noo

leg
jambe
janb

liver
foie
fwah

lungs
poumons
poo-mon

mouth
bouche
boosh

muscle
muscle
mewskl

neck
cou
koo

nose
nez
nay

skin
peau
poh

stomach
estomac
ais-toh-mah

throat
gorge
gohrj

wrist
poignet
pwahn-yay

At the dentist's

I have — a toothache
J'ai — mal aux dents
jay — mahl oh dan

— broken a tooth
— une dent cassée
— ewn dan kah-say

I have to see the dentist
Il faut que je voie le dentiste
eel foh ker jer vwah ler dan-teest

My false teeth are broken
Mon dentier est cassé
mon dan-tyay ai kah-say

My gums are sore
J'ai mal aux gencives
jay mahl oh jan-seev

Can you find out what the trouble is?
Savez-vous ce qui ne va pas?
sah-vay voo ser kee ner vah pah

Please give me an injection
Donnez-moi une piqûre, s'il vous plaît
doh-nay- mwah ewn pee-kewr, seel voo play

That hurts
Ça fait mal
sah fai mahl

At the dentist's

The filling has come out
Le plombage a sauté
ler pohm-bahj ah soh-tay

This one hurts
Celle-ci fait mal
sail-see fai mahl

Will you have to take it out?
Faudra-t-il l'arracher?
foh-drah-teel lah-rah-shay

Are you going to fill it?
Allez-vous la plomber?
ah-lay voo lah plohm-bay

ons and percentages

f un demi *an der-mee*

r un quart *an kahr*

d un tiers *an tyair*

s deux tiers *der tyair*

% dix pour *dee poor san*

y dimanche *dee-mansh*

y lundi *lern-dee*

y mardi *mahr-dee*

y mercredi *mair-krer-dee*

y jeudi *jer-dee*

y vendredi *van-drer-dee*

y samedi *sahm-dee*

FOR YOUR INFORMATION

Numbers

1 un *ern*

2 deux *der*

3 trois *trwah*

4 quatre *kahtr*

5 cinq *sank*

6 six *sees*

7 sept *sait*

8 huit *weet*

9 neuf *nerf*

10 dix *dees*

11 onze *onz*

12 douze *dooz*

13 treize *traiz*

14 quatorze *kah-tohrz*

15 quinze *kernz*

16 seize *saiz*

17 dix-sept *deez-sait*

18 dix-huit *deez-weet*

19 dix-neuf *deez-nerf*

FOR YOUR INFORMATION

Numbers

1 un *ern*

2 deux *der*

3 trois *trwah*

4 quatre *kahtr*

5 cinq *sank*

6 six *sees*

7 sept *sait*

8 huit *weet*

9 neuf *nerf*

10 dix *dees*

11 onze *onz*

12 douze *dooz*

13 treize *traiz*

14 quatorze *kah-tohrz*

15 quinze *kernz*

16 seize *saiz*

17 dix-sept *deez-sait*

18 dix-huit *deez-weet*

19 dix-neuf *deez-nerf*

Numbers

20	vingt	*vern*
21	vingt et un	*vern tay ern*
22	vingt-deux	*vernt-der*
23	vingt-trois	*vernt-trwah*
24	vingt-quatre	*vernt-kahtr*
25	vingt-cinq	*vernt-sank*
26	vingt-six	*vernt-sees*
27	vingt-sept	*vernt-sait*
28	vingt-huit	*vernt-weet*
29	vingt-neuf	*vernt-nerf*
30	trente	*trant*
40	quarante	*kah-rant*
50	cinquante	*san-kant*
60	soixante	*swah-sant*
70	soixante-dix	*swah-sant-dees*

(Belgium/Switzerland: septante *saip-tant*)

80	quatre-vingts	*kahtr-vern*

(Belgium/Switzerland: octante *ohk-tant*)

90	quatre-vingt-dix	*kahtr-vern-dees*

(Belgium/Switzerland: nonante *noh-nant*)

100	cent	*san*
200	deux cents	*der san*

Ordinals

300	trois cents *trwah san*
400	quatre cents *kahtr san*
500	cinq cents *sank san*
600	six cents *see san*
700	sept cents *sait san*
800	huit cents *wee san*
900	neuf cents *nerv san*
1000	mille *meel*
2000	deux mille *der meel*
3000	trois mille *trwah meel*
4000	quatre mille *kahtr meel*
1 000 000	un million *an mee-lyon*

Ordinals

1st	premier *prer-myay*
2nd	deuxième *der-zyaim*
3rd	troisième *trwah-zyaim*
4th	quatrième *kaht-ryaim*
5th	cinquième *sern-kyaim*
n-th	énième *ain-yaim*

Fractions and percentages

a half	un demi *an der-mee*
a quarter	un quart *an kahr*
a third	un tiers *an tyair*
two thirds	deux tiers *der tyair*
10%	dix pour *dee poor san*

Days

Sunday	dimanche *dee-mansh*
Monday	lundi *lern-dee*
Tuesday	mardi *mahr-dee*
Wednesday	mercredi *mair-krer-dee*
Thursday	jeudi *jer-dee*
Friday	vendredi *van-drer-dee*
Saturday	samedi *sahm-dee*

The seasons

Dates

on Friday	vendredi *van-drer-dee*
next Tuesday	mardi prochain *mahr-dee proh-shern*
last Tuesday	mardi dernier *mahr-dee dair-nyay*
yesterday	hier *ee-air*
today	aujourd'hui *oh-joor-dwee*
tomorrow	demain *der-mern*
next week	la semaine prochaine *lah ser-main proh-shain*
in June	en juin *an jwern*
July 7th	le sept juillet *ler sait jwee-yay*
last month	le mois dernier *ler mwah dair-nyay*

The seasons

spring	printemps *prern-tan*
summer	été *ay-tay*
autumn	automne *oh-tohn*
winter	hiver *ee-vair*

Times of the year

Times of the year

in spring	au printemps *oh prern-tan*
in summer	en été *ohn ay-tay*
in autumn	en automne *ohn oh-tohn*
in winter	en hiver *ohn ee-vair*

Months

January	janvier *jan-vyay*
February	février *fayv-ryay*
March	mars *mahrs*
April	avril *ahv-reel*
May	mai *may*
June	juin *jwern*
July	juillet *jwee-yay*
August	août *oot*
September	septembre *saip-tanbr*
October	octobre *ohk-tohbr*
November	novembre *noh-vanbr*
December	décembre *day-sanbr*

Public holidays

New Year's Day, January 1
Le Jour de l'An
ler joor der lan

Easter Monday
Le lundi de Pâques
le lern-dee der pahk

Labour Day, May 1
La Fête du Travail
lah fait dew trah-vahee

Armistice Day 1945, May 8
Le 8 mai
le wee mai

Ascension Day (40 days after Easter)
La Fête de l'Ascension
lah fait der lah-san-syon

Whit Monday (7th Monday after Easter)
La Fête de la Pentecôte
lah fait der lah pant-koht

Bastille Day, July 14
ler kah-tohrz jwee-yay

Assumption Day, August 15
La Fête de l'Assomption
la fait der lah-sohmp-syon

Public holidays

All Saints Day, November 1
La Toussaint
lah too-san

Armistice Day 1918, November 11
Le 11 novembre
ler onz noh-vanbr

Christmas Day,   December 25
Noël
noh-ail

Colours

black
noir
nwahr

blue
bleu
bler

brown
marron
mah-ron

cream
crème
kraim

fawn
fauve
fohv

gold
doré
doh-ray

green
vert
vair

grey
gris
gree

orange
orange
oh-ranj

pink
rose
rohz

purple
violet
vyoh-lay

red
rouge
rooj

silver
argenté
ahr-jan-tay

tan
ocre
ohkr

white
blanc
blan

yellow
jaune
john

Common adjectives

bad
mauvais
moh-vay

beautiful
beau/magnifique
boh/mah-nee-feek

big
grand
gran

cheap
bon marché
bon mahr-shay

cold
froid
frwah

expensive
cher
shair

difficult
difficile
dee-fee-seel

easy
facile
fah-seel

fast
rapide
rah-peed

good
bon/bien
bon/byern

high
haut
oh

hot
chaud
shoh

little
petit
per-tee

long
long
lon

new
nouveau/neuf
noo-voh/nerf

old
vieux
vee-er

Common adjectives

short
court
koor

small
petit
per-tee

slow
lent
lan

ugly
laid
lay

Signs and notices

Signs and notices

attention
caution
ah-tan-syon

ascenseur
lift/elevator
ah-san-serr

sortie
exit
sohr-tee

renseignements
information
ran-sain-man

soldes
sale
sohld

épuisé
sold out
ay-pwee-zay

occupé
occupied
oh-kew-pay

sonnez
please ring
soh-nay

poussez
push
poo-say

entrée
entrance
an-tray

entrez sans frapper
enter without knocking
an-tray san frah-pay

entrée gratuite
no admission charge
an-tray grah-tweet

téléphone
telephone
tay-lay-fohn

sapeurs-pompiers
fire brigade
sah-perr pohm-pyay

libre
vacant
leebr

Objets trouvés
Lost Property Office
ohb-jay troo-vay

Signs and notices

entrée interdite
No trespassing
an-tray ern-tair-deet

danger
danger
dan-jay

fermé
closed
fair-may

poison
poison
pwah-zon

chaud
hot
shoh

froid
cold
frwah

caisse
cashier
kais

passage interdit
no thoroughfare
pah-sahj ern-tair-dee

entrée interdite
no entry
an-tray ern-tair-deet

hôpital
hospital
oh-pee-tahl

ambulance
ambulance
an-bew-lans

chemin privé
private road
sher-mern pree-vay

piste cyclable
cycle path
peest seek-lahbl

serrez à droite
keep to the right
sai-ray ah drwaht

souvenirs
souvenirs
soov-neer

agence de voyages
travel agency
ahj-ans der voh-yahj

offre spéciale
special offer
ohfr spay-syahl

eau potable
drinking water
oh poh-tahbl

Signs and notices

déviation
diversion
day-vyah-syon

tirez
pull
tee-ray

à vendre
for sale
ah vandr

à louer
to let/for hire
ah loo-ay

tarifs
price list
tah-reef

bienvenue
welcome
byern-ver-new

réservé aux...
allowed only for
ray-sair-vay oh...

chien méchant
beware of the dog
shee-ern may-shan

police
police
poh-lees

risque d'incendie
danger of fire
reesk dern-san-dee

départs
departures
day-pahr

détritus
litter
day-tree-tews

ouvert
open
oo-vair

sonnez
ring
soh-nay

arrivées
arrivals
ah-ree-vay

école
school
ay-kohl

entrée
entrance
an-tray

horaires
timetable
oh-rair

Signs and notices

messieurs
gentlemen
may-syer

police
police
poh-lees

dames
ladies
dahm

emergency
urgence
oor-jans

customs
douane
doo-ahn

reserved
réservé
ray-sair-vay

baggage
bagages
bah-gahj

danger de mort
danger of death
dan-jay der mohr

bank
banque
bank

smoking area
espace fumeurs
ais-pahs few-merr

interdiction de marcher sur le gazon
keep off the grass
ern-tair-deek-syon der mahr-shay sewr ler gah-zon

pour usage externe seulement
for external use only
poor ew-zahj aiks-tairn serl-man

ne pas parler au conducteur en cours de route
It is forbidden to speak to the driver while the bus is moving
ner pah pahr-lay oh kon-dewk-terr an koor der root

ne pas toucher
do not touch
ner pah too-shay

Signs and notices

fire alarm
avertisseur d'incendie
ah-vair-tee-serr dern-san-dee

sortie de secours
emergency exit
sohr-tee der ser-koor

sonnette d'alarme
communication cord (rail)
soh-nait dah-lahrm

interdiction de photographier
no picture taking
ern-tair-deek-syon der foh-toh-grah-fyay

réservé au personnel
employees only
ray-sair-vay oh pair-soh-nail

parking réservé aux résidents
parking for residents only
pahr-keeng ray-sair-vay oh ray-zee-dan

compartiment fumeurs
smoking compartment
kohm-pahr-tee-man few-merr

liquidation des stocks
closing-down sale
lee-kee-dah-syon day stohk

fermé l'après-midi
closed in the afternoon
fair-may lah-prai-mee-dee

Signs and notices

ne pas se pencher au dehors
do not lean out
ner pah ser pan-shay oh der-ohr

interdiction de fumer
no smoking
ern-tair-deek-syon der few-may

In an Emergency

Call — an ambulance
Appelez — une ambulance.
ah-play — ewn an-bew-lans

— the fire brigade
— les pompiers.
— lay pohm-pyay

— the police
— la police
— lah poh-lees

There is a fire
Il y a un incendie.
eel-yah ern ern-san-dee

Get a doctor
Appelez un médecin.
ah-play ern mayd-sern

My daughter is ill
Ma fille est malade.
mah fee ai mah-lahd

My son is lost
Mon fils s'est perdu.
mon fees sai pair-dew

Who speaks English?
Qui parle anglais?
kee pahrl an-glay?

Where is the British consulate?
Où se trouve le consulat de Grande-Bretagne?
oo ser troov ler kon-sew-lah der grand-brer-tahn?